AF838564

FUNDAMENTALS OF
BUSINESS LAW

FUNDAMENTALS OF
BUSINESS LAW

– Author –
Vidur Chander
Aditya Singh

Wordpen Academics
Publishing Science That Matter

© 2025 PUBLISHER

Information contained in this work has been published by Wordpen Academics and has been obtained by its author(s)/editor(s) from sources believed to be reliable and are correct to the best of their knowledge. However, the publisher and its author(s) make no representation of warranties with respect of accuracy or completeness of the contents of this book, and shall in no event be liable for any errors, omissions or damages arising out of use of this information and specifically disclaim any implied warranties or merchantability or fitness for any particular purpose.

All rights reserved. Including the right to translate or to reproduce this book or parts thereof except for brief quotations in critical reviews.

ISBN: 978-93-6084-933-7

Published by : WORDPEN ACADEMICS
4736/23, Ansari Road, Darya Ganj,
New Delhi – 110 002
Phone: +91-011-35004336
E-mail: info@wordpenacademics.com

Exclusive Distributor: ***Bio-Green Books, New Delhi***

Preface

Business law refers to a set of laws that govern the establishment, operation, and dissolution of businesses. It encompasses a broad range of legal issues, such as contracts, property rights, intellectual property, employment law, and taxation. Understanding business law is essential for anyone who wants to start, operate, or invest in a business. One of the most important aspects of business law is contract law. Contracts are legal agreements that outline the terms and conditions of a business transaction. They establish the rights and obligations of the parties involved and provide a framework for resolving disputes. A contract can be verbal or written, but written contracts are preferred because they provide a clear record of the agreement. Another important aspect of business law is property law. Property law governs the ownership, use, and transfer of property. It includes real property (land and buildings), personal property (such as cars and furniture), and intellectual property (such as patents, trademarks, and copyrights). Businesses must comply with property law when acquiring, using, and selling property.

Intellectual property law is particularly important for businesses that rely on intellectual property to generate revenue. Patents protect inventions, trademarks protect brands, and copyrights protect creative works. Businesses that fail to protect their intellectual property risk losing their competitive advantage and may face legal action from competitors. Employment law is another crucial area of business law. It governs the employer-employee relationship and includes issues such as discrimination, harassment, and wrongful termination. Businesses must comply with employment laws to avoid legal liability and maintain a positive workplace culture. In addition to these areas, there are many other legal issues that businesses may face. For example, businesses must comply with environmental regulations, antitrust laws, and consumer protection laws. They may also face legal disputes with customers, suppliers, or competitors. To navigate these complex legal issues, businesses often rely on the expertise of lawyers and other legal professionals. They may also consult with accountants and other financial experts to ensure compliance with tax laws and financial reporting requirements. Business law is a crucial area of law that governs the establishment, operation, and dissolution of businesses. Understanding business law is essential for anyone who wants to start, operate, or invest in a business. It is a complex area of law that encompasses many different legal issues, including contract law, property law, intellectual property law, employment law, and taxation. To navigate these issues, businesses often rely on the expertise of lawyers and other legal professionals.

It covers American Law, Legal Reasoning, and the Legal System, providing an introduction to the legal framework in the United States and discusses Disputes and Dispute Settlement. The book covers Business Ethics and Social Responsibility, emphasizing the importance of ethical business practices and corporate social responsibility and discusses Criminal Liability, including the different types of criminal offenses and their consequences. The book covers Contract Law, including the elements of a valid contract, breach of contract, and remedies for breach and discusses Sales Contracts and the legal requirements for their formation and enforcement. Employment and Labor Law is explored, including the various laws that regulate the employment relationship, such as anti-discrimination laws and minimum wage laws and also covers Government Regulation, such as environmental regulations and safety regulations. Antitrust Law is discussed, including the laws that promote competition and prevent monopolies. The book covers Unfair Trade Practices and the Federal Trade Commission, including the laws that prohibit unfair and deceptive business practices and the role of the FTC in enforcing these laws. International Law is explored, including the different sources of international law and the legal implications for businesses that operate across borders. Securities Regulation is discussed, including the laws that regulate the sale and purchase of securities and the legal requirements for companies that issue securities. This book is primarily targeted at business students, entrepreneurs, and legal professionals and also covers a wide range of topics that are essential for anyone who wants to understand the legal implications of their business decisions.

We are grateful to all those persons as well as various books, manuals, periodicals, magazines, journals etc. that helped in the preparation of this book. In spite of the best efforts, it is possible that some errors may have occurred into the compilation and editing of the book. Further queries, constructive suggestions and criticisms for the improvement of the book are always welcomed and shall be thankfully acknowledged.

Vidur Chander
Aditya Singh

Contents

Preface .... *v*

1. **American Law, Legal Reasoning, and the Legal System** 3
   - Basic American Legal Principles
   - Sources and Types of Law
   - Important Business Laws and Regulations
2. **Disputes and Dispute Settlement** 15
   - Negotiation
   - Mediation
   - Arbitration
   - Arbitration Awards
3. **Business Ethics and Social Responsibility** 31
   - Business Ethics
   - Social Responsibility
4. **Business and the United States Constitution** 42
   - Commerce Clause
   - Police Power and the Dormant Commerce Clause
   - Constitutional Protections
5. **Criminal Liability** 53
   - Common Business Crimes
   - Types of Business Crimes
   - Civil vs. Criminal Liability
6. **The Tort System** 63
   - Intentional Torts and Negligence
   - Product and Strict Liability
   - The Unreasonably Dangerous Product Standard

7. **Contract Law** 75
- Consideration and Promissory Estoppel
- Capacity and Legality
- Breach of Contract and Remedies

8. **Sales Contracts** 85
- The Nature and Origins of Sales Contracts
- Warranties and Sales Contracts
- Breaches of Warranty

09. **Employment and Labor Law** 97
- Employment, Worker Protection, and Immigration Law
- Labor Law
- Equal Opportunity in Employment

10. **Government Regulation** 111
- Administrative Law
- Regulatory Agencies

11. **Antitrust Law** 123
- History of Antitrust Law
- Unfair Business Practices
- Antitrust Laws

12. **Unfair Trade Practices and the Federal Trade Commission** 132
- Unfair Trade Practices
- The Federal Trade Commission

13. **International Law** 140
- Introduction to International Law
- Sources and Practice of International Law
- Impact on International Trade

14. **Securities Regulation** 151
- Liability Under the Securities Act
- The Framework of Securities Regulation
- The SEC

Index 165

1 American Law, Legal Reasoning, and the Legal System

Figure 1.1 (Credit: MarkThomas /pixabay /Attribution 2.0 Generic (CC BY 2.0))

Chapter Outline

1.1 Basic American Legal Principles
1.2 Sources and Types of Law
1.3 Important Business Laws and Regulations

Introduction

Learning Outcome

- Describe the foundation and sources that establish American law.

1.1 Basic American Legal Principles

The American legal system has its roots in the British legal system. It was developed with the purpose of establishing standards for acceptable conduct, proscribing punishment for violations as a deterrent, establishing systems for enforcement, and peacefully resolving disputes. The ultimate goal of the American legal system is promotion of the common good.

Establishing Standards

The American legal system was developed with the goal of establishing a set of standards that outline what is to be considered minimally acceptable behavior. Broadly speaking, federal laws are those that all United States citizens are expected to follow. State and local laws may often be similar to federal laws, but they may also differ quite a bit, and only govern the state's citizens.

Figure 1.2 The American legal system is designed to establish a set of standards for acceptable behavior. (Credit: joergelman/ pixabay/ License: CC0)

Promoting Consistency

The American legal system follows the British Common Law system, which is designed to leverage past judicial reasoning, while also promoting fairness through consistency. Judges in the Common Law system help shape the law through their rulings and interpretations. This body of past decisions is known as **case law**. Judges use case law to inform their own rulings. Indeed, judges rely on **precedent**, i.e., previous court rulings on similar cases, for ruling on their own cases.

All U.S. states, except Louisiana, have enacted "reception statutes," stating that the judge-made common law of England is the law of the state to the extent that it does not conflict with the state's current laws.

However, the body of American law is now so robust that American cases rarely cite English materials, except for a British classic or a famous old case. Additionally, foreign law is not cited as binding precedent. Therefore, the current American practice of the common law tradition refers more to the process of judges looking to the precedent set jurisdictionally, and substantially similar to, American case law.

Maintaining Order

Congruent with the goal of establishing standards and promoting consistency, laws are also used to promote, provide, and maintain order.

Resolving Disputes

Conflicts are to be expected given people's varying needs, desires, objectives, values systems, and perspectives. The American legal system provides a formal means for resolving conflicts through the courts. In addition to the federal court and individual state systems, there are also several informal means for resolving disputes that are collectively called alternative dispute resolution (ADR). Examples of these are mediation and arbitration.

Protecting Liberties and Rights

The United States Constitution and state laws provide people with many liberties and rights. American laws operate with the purpose and function of protecting these liberties and rights from violations by persons, companies, governments, or other entities.

Based on the British legal system, the American legal system is divided into a federal system and a state and local system. The overall goal of both systems is to provide order and a means of dispute settlement, as well as to protect citizens' rights.

Clearly, the purposes of the American legal system are broad and well-considered.

1.2 Sources and Types of Law

The American legal system is made up of many types of codified forms of law, with the United States Constitution being the pre-eminent source of American law. The Constitution establishes the boundaries of federal law, and it must be followed by all citizens, organizations, and entities. It includes Congressional acts, Senate-ratified treaties, executive regulations, and federal case law. The United States Code ("USC") compiles these laws.

American law mainly originates from constitutional law, statutory law, treaties, administrative regulations, and common law (which includes case law).

The Constitution

The United States Constitution is the foremost law of the land. The Constitution's first ten amendments are referred to as the Bill of Rights, which offers specific protections of individual liberty and justice. Additionally, the Bill of Rights restricts certain powers of government. The Constitution empowers federal law making by giving Congress the power to enact statutes for certain limited purposes, like regulating interstate commerce. The United States Code officially compiles and codifies the federal statutes.

Figure 1.3 The U.S. Constitution is known as the supreme law of the land. (Credit: lynn0101/ pixabay/ License: CC0)

American Common Law

As discussed in the previous section, the United States follows the common law legal tradition of English law. Judges in the Common Law system help shape the law through their rulings and interpretations. This body of past decisions is known as **case law**, which is used by judges to inform their own rulings. In fact, judges rely on **precedent**, i.e., previous court rulings on similar cases, when determining the ruling in their own cases.

An example of how case law works is the case of the State v. Wayfair Inc. (2017 SD 56, 901 N.W.2d 754 (S.D. 2017), cert. granted, 138 S. Ct. 735 (2018)), in which the South Dakota Supreme Court held that a state law requiring internet retailers without an in-state physical presence to remit sales tax was unconstitutional. Unless this ruling is overruled by the United States Supreme Court, then it becomes part of the case law and precedent set in that state, and it will be followed by subsequent rulings when similar cases are filed.

Federal Law

The Constitution empowers federal law making by giving Congress the power to enact statutes for certain limited purposes, like regulating interstate commerce. Federal law preempts conflicting state and local laws. However, federal preemption is not without limits, insofar as states each have their own constitution and are considered sovereign. Therefore, federal law may only preempt state law if it is enacted within the limited powers that are enumerated and granted to Congress in the Constitution.

Broad interpretations of the Constitution's Commerce and Spending Clauses have expanded the reach of federal law into many areas. Indeed, its reach in some areas, such as aviation and railroads, is now so broad that it preempts virtually all state law. In others areas, such as family law, lawmaking continues to be left to the states. Finally, a number of powerful federal and state laws coexist in areas such as antitrust, trademark, employment law, and others.

Statutes

When a bill becomes a federal law, it is assigned a law number and prepared for publication by the Office of the Federal Register (OFR) of the National Archives and Records Administration (NARA). Public laws are also given legal statutory citation by the OFR and are incorporated into the United States Code (USC).

Regulations

Laws differ from regulations in that laws are passed by either the U.S. Congress or state congresses. Regulations, by contrast, are standards and rules adopted by administrative agencies that govern how laws will be enforced.

Federal agencies often enjoy broad rulemaking authority when Congress acts to grant them this power. Called "regulations," these agency rules normally carry the force of law, as long as they demonstrate a reasonable interpretation of the relevant statutes. For example, the Environmental Protection Agency (EPA) has established regulations for businesses and their emission and disposal of pollutants to protect the environment. The EPA has the authority to enforce these regulations when a business violates them, and such enforcement is usually done by fining the company or by using other means.

The Administrative Procedure Act (APA) enables the adoption of regulations, which are codified and incorporated into the Code of Federal Regulations (CFR). Federal agencies frequently draft and distribute forms, manuals, policy statements, letters, and rulings. Though these may be considered as persuasive authority by the courts, they do not carry the same force as law. In other words, if a person or business questions a regulation of a government agency, saying it is unconstitutional, and that party is successful in proving it, then the regulation is not enforced and the agency will need to revise it or remove it.

State Law

America, as diverse as its fifty states, is also governed by fifty different state constitutions, state governments, and state courts. Each has its own legislative, executive, and judicial branches. States are empowered to create legislation that is related to matters not preempted by the federal Constitution and federal laws. Most cases involve state law issues and are litigated in state courts.

Local Law

In addition to federal and state law, municipalities, towns or cities, and counties may enact their own laws that do not conflict with state or federal laws.

As demonstrated, American law does not draw from one source alone; instead, it is derived from many sources.

1.3 Important Business Laws and Regulations

Business law is a very expansive area of the law. It primarily addresses issues related to the creation of new businesses, which arise as existing companies deal with the public, government, and other companies.

Business law consists of many legal disciplines, including contracts, tax law, corporate law, intellectual property, real estate, sales, immigration law, employment law, bankruptcy, and others.

Figure 1.4 Contract law is just one type of law that businesses need to be concerned about. (Credit: edar/ pixabay/ License: CC0)

As noted, business law touches upon a number of other legal areas, practices, and concerns. Some of the most important of these, which are discussed in this section, are disputes and dispute settlement, business ethics and social responsibility, business and the United States Constitution, criminal liability, torts, contracts, labor and employment law, Unfair Trade Practices and the Federal Trade Commission, international law, and securities regulation. Though they are discussed in much more depth in later chapters, the following gives a brief overview.

Disputes and Dispute Settlement

In addition to the federal court and individual state systems, there are also a variety of mechanisms that companies can use to resolve disputes. They are collectively called alternative dispute resolution ("ADR"), and they include mediation, settlement, and arbitration. Many states now require companies to resolve legal disputes using ADR before the initiation of any lawsuit to encourage speedy resolution, cost and time containment, and reduced judicial dockets. Traditional litigation remains an option in most cases if other efforts fail or are refused.

Business Ethics and Social Responsibility

In the routine course of business, employees are often required to make decisions. Business ethics outline the ethical model, or framework, that companies expect employees to follow when making these decisions, as well as the behavior that the companies deem acceptable. Sound and ethical decision making can also help companies avoid legal liability and exposure. Typically, an ethics code and/or a code of conduct details a company's requirements and guidelines, while also serving as a key corporate governance tool.

In addition to business ethics, companies must also consider their social responsibility and the laws related to it, such as consumer and investor protections, environmental ethics, marketing ethics, and ethical issues in financial management.

Business and the United States Constitution

Since the start of the 20th century, broad interpretations of the Constitution's Commerce and Spending Clauses have expanded the reach of federal law into many areas. Indeed, its reach in some areas is now so broad that it preempts virtually all state law. Thus, the Constitution's Commerce Clause has been interpreted to allow federal lawmaking and enforcement that applies to many aspects of business activity. Additionally, the Constitution's Bill of Rights extends some protections to business entities that are also constitutionally guaranteed to individuals

For example, on January 21, 2010, in Citizens United v. Federal Election Commission, 558 U.S. 310 (2010), the U.S. Supreme Court heard the issue of whether the government can ban political spending by corporations in candidate elections. The Court ruled that corporations have the same Constitutional right to free speech as individuals, and thus lifted the restrictions on contributions.

Criminal Liability

The imposition of criminal liability is one method used to regulate companies. The extent of corporate liability found in an offensive act determines whether a company will be held liable for the acts and omissions of its employees. Criminal consequences may include penalties, such as prison, fines and/or community service. In addition to criminal liability, civil law remedies are usually available, e.g., the award of damages and injunctions, which may include penalties. Most jurisdictions apply both criminal and civil systems.

Torts

Within the business law context, torts may involve either intentional torts or negligence. Additionally, companies involved in certain industries should consider the risk of product liability. Product liability involves a legal action against a company by a consumer for a defective product that caused loss or harm to the customer. There are several theories regarding recovery under product liability. These include contract theories that deal with the product warranty, which details the promises of the nature of the product sold to customers. The contract product warranty theories are Express Warranty, Implied Warranty of Merchantability, and Implied Warranty of Fitness. Tort theories deal with a consumer claim that the company was negligent, and therefore caused either bodily harm, emotional harm, or monetary loss to the plaintiff. The tort liability theories that can be used in this context are negligence (failure to take proper care in something), strict liability (imposition of liability without a finding of fault), and acts committed under Restatement (Third) of Torts (basic elements of the tort action for liability for accidental personal injury and property damage, as well as liability for emotional harm).

Contracts

The main function of a contract is to document promises that are enforceable by law. The key to an agreement or contract is that there must be an offer and acceptance of the terms of that offer. Sales contracts normally involve the sale of goods and include price terms, quantity and cost, how the terms of the contract will be performed, and method of delivery.

Employment and Labor Law

Employment and labor law is a very broad discipline that covers a broad array of laws and regulations involving employer/employee rights and responsibilities in the workplace. This law includes worker protection and safety laws, such as OSHA, and worker immigration laws, such as the Immigration Reform and Control Act, which imposes sanctions on employers for knowingly hiring illegal immigrants. Other notable areas of employment and labor law include, but are not limited to, the National Labor Relations Act, which deals with union and management relations, as well as Equal Opportunity in Employment laws, which provide workers with protections against discrimination in the workplace, e.g., Title VII, the Americans with Disabilities Act, Age Discrimination in Employment Act, and others.

Antitrust Law

Antitrust legislation includes both federal and state laws regulating companies' conduct and organization. The purpose of such regulation is to allow consumers to benefit from the promotion of fair competition. The main statutes implicated by antitrust law are the Sherman Act of 1890, the Clayton Act of 1914, and the Federal Trade Commission Act of 1914. These Acts discourage the restraint of trade by prohibiting the creation of cartels and other collusive practices. Additionally, they encourage competition by restricting the mergers and acquisitions of certain organizations. Finally, they prohibit the creation and abuse of monopoly power.

Actions may be brought in courts to enforce antitrust laws by the Federal Trade Commission ("FTC"), the U.S. Department of Justice, state governments, and private parties.

Unfair Trade Practices and the Federal Trade Commission

The term "unfair trade practices" is broadly used and refers to any deceptive or fraudulent business practice or act that causes injury to a consumer. Some examples include, but are not limited to, false representations of a good or service including deceptive pricing, non-compliance with manufacturing standards, and false advertising. The FTC investigates allegations of unfair trade practices raised by consumers and businesses, pre-merger notification filings, congressional inquiries, or reports in the media and may seek voluntary compliance by offending businesses through a consent order, administrative complaints, or federal litigation.

Securities Regulation

Securities regulation involves both federal and state regulation of securities and stocks by governmental regulatory agencies. At times, it may also involve the regulations of exchanges like the New York Stock Exchange, as well as the rules of self-regulatory organizations like the Financial Industry Regulatory Authority (FINRA).

The Securities and Exchange Commission (SEC) regulates securities on the federal level. Other instruments related to securities, such as futures and some derivatives, are regulated by the Commodity Futures Trading Commission (CFTC).

Assessment Questions

1. What country is the United States legal system derived from?

a. Germany.
b. United Kingdom.
c. United States of America.
d. Canada.

2. What is the function of law in the United States?

a. Establish standards.
b. Promote consistency.
c. Promote, provide, and maintain order.
d. All of the above.

3. As a judge, Baxter applies common law rules. These rules develop from:

a. decisions of the courts in legal disputes.
b. regulations issued by administrative agencies.
c. statutes enacted by Congress and the state legislatures.
d. uniform laws drafted by legal scholars.

4. What is the difference between state and federal law?

5. The legislature of the state of Wyoming enacts a new statute that sets standards for the liability of businesses selling defective products. This statute applies in:

a. Wyoming only.
b. only Wyoming and its bordering states.
c. all states.
d. all states but only to matters not covered by other states' laws.

6. Alex has been sued by Will for failure to pay rent for their apartment which source of law will govern this lawsuit?

a. Administrative law.
b. The Constitution.
c. Civil Law.
d. Criminal Law.

7. Four sources of law in the U.S. legal system are:

a. Constitutional law, criminal law, civil law, and maritime law.
b. Federal law, state law, international law, and maritime law.
c. Statutory law, case law, equity, and common law.
d. Constitutional law, judicial law, legislative law, and administrative law.

8. Where can you find a codification of federal laws?

a. The library.
b. Federal Court.
c. United States Code.
d. U.S. Library of Congress.

9. What is the supreme law of the land? What are statutes? What are ordinances? What is an administrative rule?

10. Regulations are:

a. Laws passed by Congress.
b. Rules made by local governments.
c. Derived from decisions made by judges.
d. Rules adopted by administrative agencies.

11. What is an Unfair Trade Practice and which Administrative Agency regulates it?

12. Some of the rights in the Constitution's Bill of Rights extends to Corporations.

a. True.
b. False.

13. Forms of Alternative Dispute Resolution ("ADR") include all of the following except:

a. Mediation.
b. Settlement.
c. Litigation.
d. Arbitration.

14. Consequences of being convicted a crime include all of the following except:

a. Prison.
b. Fines.
c. Community service.
d. Damages.

15. Securities are only regulated by federal laws.

a. True.
b. False.

Endnotes

Overview – Rule of Law. United States Courts. Retrieved from: www.uscourts.gov/educational-resources/educational-activities/overview-rule-law.

Purposes and Functions of Business Law. UpCounsel. Retrieved from: https://www.upcounsel.com/purposes-and-functions-of-business-law.

Williams, L. and Lumen Learning. The Meaning and Purposes of Law. Lumen Learning – Introduction to Business. Retrieved from: https://courses.lumenlearning.com/wmopen-introbusiness/chapter/meaning-and-purposes-of-the-law/.

Feltes, G. A Guide to the U.S. Federal Legal System - Web-based Public Accessible Sources. 2005. Hauser Global Law School Program. Retrieved from: http://www.nyulawglobal.org/globalex/United_States.html.

How Laws Are Made. GovTrack. Retrieved from: https://www.govtrack.us/what-is-the-law.

Public Laws. December 28, 2017. National Archives. Retrieved from: https://www.archives.gov/federal-register/laws.

Steenken, B. & Brooks, T. The United States Legal System. Sources of Law. Retrieved from: http://sourcesofamericanlaw.lawbooks.cali.org/chapter/the-united-states-legal-system/.

Business Law Courses. edX. Retrieved from: https://www.edx.org/learn/business-law.

This OpenStax book is available for free at http://cnx.org/content/col30149/1.5

Introductory Business Law. Modern States. Retrieved from: https://modernstates.org/course/introductory-business-law/.

2 Disputes and Dispute Settlement

Figure 2.1 (Credit: rawpixel/ pixabay/ Attribution 2.0 Generic (CC BY 2.0))

Chapter Outline

2.1 Negotiation
2.2 Mediation
2.3 Arbitration

Introduction

Learning Outcome

- Explain the theory, practice, and law of disputes and resolution.

2.1 Negotiation

We frequently engage in negotiations as we go about our daily activities, often without being consciously aware that we are doing so. Negotiation can be simple, e.g., two friends deciding on a place to eat dinner, or complex, e.g., governments of several nations trying to establish import and export quotas across multiple industries. When a formal proceeding is started in the court system, **alternative dispute resolution** (**ADR**), or ways of solving an issue with the intent to avoid **litigation**, may be employed. Negotiation is often the first step used in ADR. While there are other forms of alternative dispute resolution, negotiation is considered to be the simplest because it does not require outside parties. An article in the **Organization Behavior and Human Decision Processes** defined **negotiation** as the "process by which parties with nonidentical preferences allocate resources through interpersonal activity and joint decision making." Analyzing the various components of this definition is helpful in understanding the theories and practices involved in negotiation as a form of dispute settlement.

Negotiation Types and Objectives

Per the above definition, negotiation becomes necessary when two parties hold "non-identical" preferences. This statement seems fairly obvious, since 100% agreement would indicate that there is not any need for negotiation. From this basic starting point, there are several ways of thinking about negotiation, including how many parties are involved. For example, if two small business owners find themselves in a disagreement over property lines, they will frequently engage in **dyadic negotiation**. Put simply, dyadic negotiation involves two individuals interacting with one another in an attempt to resolve a dispute. If a third neighbor overhears the dispute and believes one or both of them are wrong with regard to the property line, then **group negotiation** could ensue. Group negotiation involves more than two individuals or parties, and by its very nature, it is often more complex, time-consuming, and challenging to resolve.

While dyadic and group negotiations may involve different dynamics, one of the most important aspects of any negotiation, regardless of the quantity of negotiators, is the objective. Negotiation experts recognize two major goals of negotiation: relational and outcome. **Relational goals** are focused on building, maintaining, or repairing a partnership, connection, or rapport with another party. **Outcome goals**, on the other hand, concentrate on achieving certain end results. The goal of any negotiation is influenced by numerous factors, such as whether or not there will be contact with the other party in the future. For example, when a business negotiates with a supply company that it intends to do business with in the foreseeable future, it will try to focus on "win-win" solutions that provide the most value for each party. In contrast, if an interaction is of a one-time nature, that same company might approach a supplier with a "win-lose" mentality, viewing its objective as maximizing its own value at the expense of the other party's value. This approach is referred to as **zero-sum negotiation**, and it is considered to be a "hard" negotiating style. Zero-sum negotiation is based on the notion that there is a "fixed pie," and the larger the slice that one party receives, the smaller the slice the other party will receive. Win-win approaches to negotiation are sometimes referred to as **integrative**, while win-lose approaches are called **distributive**.

Figure 2.2 Certain negotiation styles adopt a mindset in which the extent of one's win is proportional to the other's loss. (Credit: Sebastian Voortman/ pexels/ License: CC0)

Negotiation Style

Everyone has a different way of approaching negotiation, depending on the circumstance and the person's personality. However, the **Thomas-Kilmann Conflict Mode Instrument (TKI)** is a questionnaire that provides a systematic framework for categorizing five broad negotiation styles. It is closely associated with work done by conflict resolution experts Dean Pruitt and Jeffrey Rubin. These styles are often considered in terms of the level of self-interest, instead of how other negotiators feel. These five general negotiation styles include:

- **Forcing**. If a party has high concern for itself, and low concern for the other party, it may adopt a competitive approach that only takes into account the outcomes it desires. This negotiation style is most prone to zero-sum thinking. For example, a car dealership that tries to give each customer as little as possible for his or her trade-in vehicle would be applying a forcing negotiation approach. While the party using the forcing approach is only considering its own self-interests, this negotiating style often undermines the party's long-term success. For example, in the car dealership example, if a customer feels she has not received a fair trade-in value after the sale, she may leave negative reviews and will not refer her friends and family to that dealership and will not return to it when the time comes to buy another car.
- **Collaborating**. If a party has high concern and care for both itself and the other party, it will often employ a collaborative negotiation that seeks to maximum the gain for both. In this negotiating style, parties recognize that acting in their mutual interests may create greater value and synergies.
- **Compromising**. A compromising approach to negotiation will take place when parties share some concerns for both themselves and the other party. While it is not always possible to collaborate, parties can often find certain points that are more important to one versus the other, and in that way, find ways to isolate what is most important to each party.
- **Avoiding**. When a party has low concern for itself and for the other party, it will often try to avoid negotiation completely.
- **Yielding**. Finally, when a party has low self-concern for itself and high concern for the other party, it will yield to demands that may not be in its own best interest. As with avoidance techniques, it is important to ask why the party has low self-concern. It may be due to an unfair power differential between the two parties that has caused the weaker party to feel it is futile to represent its own interests. This example illustrates why negotiation is often fraught with ethical issues.

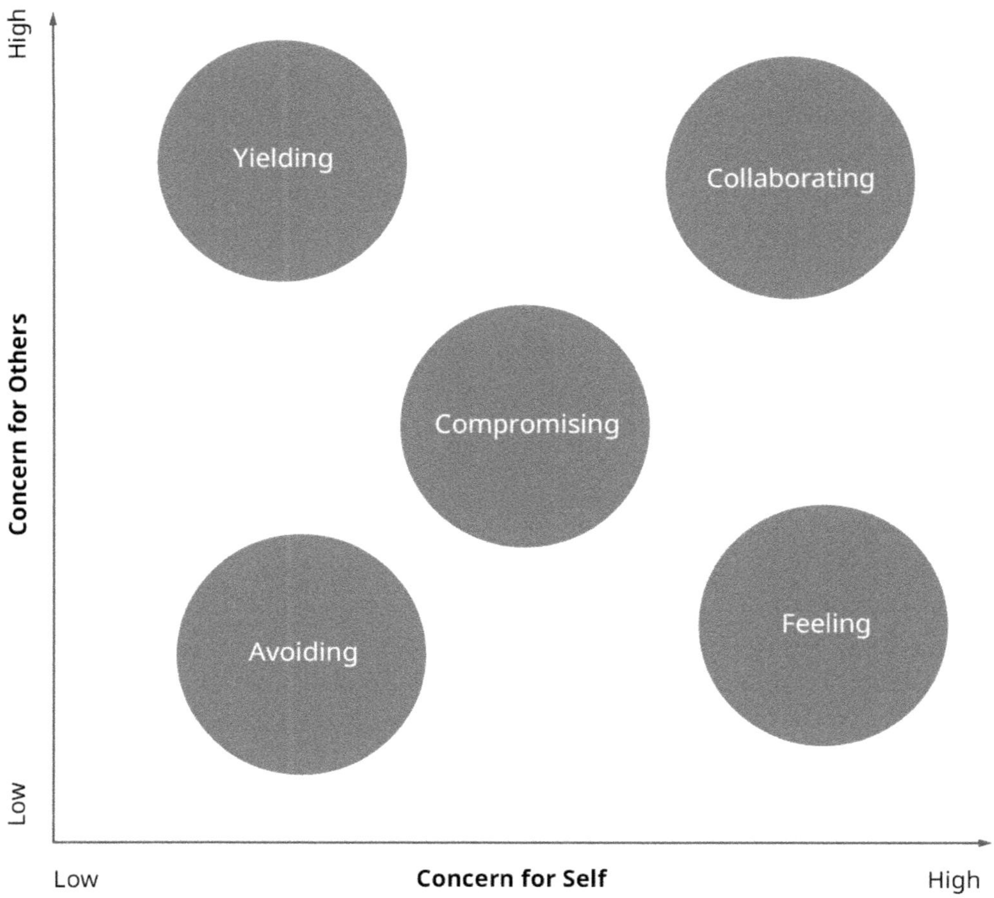

Figure 2.3 Concern for self vs. others leads to the differences in negotiating styles. (Modification of art by BNED/Rubin Credit: CC BY NC SA)

Negotiation Styles in Practice

Apple's response to its treatment of warranties in China, i.e., giving one-year warranties instead of two-year warranties as required by law, serves as an example of how negotiation may be used. While Apple products continued to be successful and popular in China, the issue rankled its customers, and Chinese celebrities joined the movement to address the concern. Chinese consumers felt that Apple was arrogant and didn't value its customers or the customers' feedback. In response, Tim Cook issued a public apology in which he expressed regret over the misunderstanding, saying, "We are aware that insufficient communications during this process has led to the perception that Apple is arrogant and disregards, or pays little attention to, consumer feedback. We express our sincere apologies for any concern or misunderstanding arising therefrom." Apple then listed four ways it intended to resolve the matter. By exhibiting humility and concern for its customers, Apple was able to diffuse a contentious situation that might have resulted in costly litigation.

Negotiation Laws

Negotiations are covered by a medley of federal and state laws, such as the **Federal Arbitration Act** and **Uniform Arbitration Act**. The Federal Arbitration Act (FAA) is a national policy that favors arbitration and enforces situations in which parties have contractually agreed to participate in arbitration. Parties who have decided to be subject to binding arbitration relinquish their constitutional right to settle their dispute in court. It is the FAA that allows parties to confirm their awards, as will be discussed in the following chapters. When considering negotiation laws, it is important to keep in mind that each state has laws with their own definitions and nuances. While the purpose of the Uniform Arbitration Act in the United States was to provide a uniform approach to the way states handle arbitration, it has only been adopted in some form by about 35 states.

2.2 Mediation

Court or Agency-Connected Mediation

Mediation is a method of dispute resolution that relies on an impartial third-party decision-maker, known as a **mediator**, to settle a dispute. While requirements vary by state, a mediator is someone who has been trained in conflict resolution, though often, he or she does not have any expertise in the subject matter that is being disputed. Mediation is another form of alternative dispute resolution. It is often used in attempts to resolve a dispute because it can help disagreeing parties avoid the time-consuming and expensive procedures involved in court litigation. Courts will often recommend that a **plaintiff**, or the party initiating a lawsuit, and a **defendant**, or the party that is accused of wrongdoing, attempt mediation before proceeding to trial. This recommendation is especially true for issues that are filed in small claims courts, where judges attempt to streamline dispute resolution. Not all mediators are associated with public court systems. There are many agency-connected and private mediation services that disputing parties can hire to help them potentially resolve their dispute. The American Bar Association suggests that, in addition to training courses, one of the best ways to start a private mediation business is to volunteer as a mediator. Research has shown that experience is an important factor for mediators who are seeking to cultivate sensitivity and hone their conflict resolution skills.

For businesses, the savings associated with mediation can be substantial. For example, the energy corporation Chevron implemented an internal mediation program. In one instance, it cost $25,000 to resolve a dispute using this internal mediation program, far less than the estimated $700,000 it would have incurred through the use of outside legal services. Even more impressive is the amount it saved by not going to court, which would have cost an estimated $2.5 million.

Mediation is distinguished by its focus on solutions. Instead of focusing on discoveries, testimonies, and expert witnesses to assess what has happened in the past, it is future-oriented. Mediators focus on discovering ways to solve the dispute in a way that will appease both parties.

Other Benefits of Mediation

- **Confidentiality**. Since court proceedings become a matter of public record, it can be advantageous to use mediation to preserve anonymity. This aspect can be especially important when dealing with sensitive matters, where one or both parties feels it is best to keep the situation private.
- **Creativity**. Mediators are trained to find ways to resolve disputes and may apply outside-the-box thinking to suggest a resolution that the parties had not considered. Since disagreeing parties can be feeling emotionally contentious toward one another, they may not be able to consider other solutions. In addition, a skilled mediator may be able to recognize cultural differences between the parties that are influencing the parties' ability to reach a compromise, and thus leverage this awareness to create a novel solution.
- **Control**. When a case goes to trial, both parties give up a certain degree of control over the outcome. A

judge may come up with a solution to which neither party is in favor. In contrast, mediation gives the disputing parties opportunities to find common ground on their own terms, before relinquishing control to outside forces.

Role of the Mediator

Successful mediators work to immediately establish personal rapport with the disputing parties. They often have a short period of time to interact with the parties and work to position themselves as a trustworthy advisor. The Harvard Law School Program on Negotiation reports a study by mediator Peter Adler in which mediation participants remembered the mediators as "opening the room, making coffee, and getting everyone introduced." This quote underscores the need for mediators to play a role beyond mere administrative functions. The mediator's conflict resolution skills are critical in guiding the parties toward reaching a resolution.

Steps of Mediation

As explained by nolo.com (http://nolo.com) , mediation, while not being as formal as a court trial, involves the following six steps:

- **Mediator's Opening Statement**: During the opening statement, the mediator introduces himself or herself and explains the goals of mediation.
- **Opening Statements of Plaintiff and Defendant**: Both parties are given the opportunity to speak, without interruption. During this opening statement, both parties are afforded the opportunity to describe the nature of the dispute and their desired solution.
- **Joint Discussion**: The mediator will try to get the two disagreeing parties to speak to one another and will guide the discussion toward a mutually amicable solution. This part of the mediation process usually identifies which issues need to be resolved and explores ways to address the issues.
- **Private Caucus**: During this stage, each party has the ability to meet and speak privately with the mediator. Typically, the mediator will use this time to learn more about what is most important to each party and to brainstorm ways to find a resolution. The mediator may ask the parties to try to put aside their emotional responses and resentments to work toward an agreement.
- **Joint Negotiation**: After the private caucuses, the parties are joined again in the same room, and the mediator presents any newly discovered insight to guide them toward an agreement.
- **Closure**: During this final stage, an agreement is reached, or it is determined that the parties cannot agree. Either way, the mediator will review the positions of each party and ask them if they would like to meet again or explore escalating options, such as moving the dispute to court.

Ethical Issues

Both the disputants themselves, and those who attempt to facilitate dispute resolutions, i.e., mediators and attorneys, must navigate a myriad of ethical issues, such as deciding whether they should tell the entire truth, or only offer a partial disclosure. This conflict has long roots in history and has often been considered in terms of consequentialist and deontological ethical theories. **Consequentialist ethics**, sometimes known as situational ethics, is a way of looking at difficult decisions by considering their implications. Someone who follows consequentialist ethics in mediation or arbitration would consider the impact of his or her decision on the parties in light of their unique circumstances. In contrast, **deontologist ethics** bases its decision on whether the action itself is right or wrong, regardless of its consequences.

Imagine a situation in which a professional accountant holds a consequentialist ethical viewpoint and believes that there are certain scenarios in which the disclosure of only part of the truth is a commendable course of action. For example, if an accountant is interviewed regarding how the company handled a certain transaction in its retirement account, he might choose to withhold certain information because he is afraid it will harm the retirees' ability to retain the full benefits of their pensions. In this case, the accountant is utilizing "the ends justify the means" logic because he feels that the omission of truth will result in more benefit than its revelation. A mediator or arbitrator who also follows a consequentialist viewpoint would consider the accountant's motivation and the circumstances, in addition to his or her actions.

Ethical situations like these are not only part of dispute mediation in business law scenarios, but also happen in daily life. Consider the case of a parent who is on his way home from work when he receives a call from the babysitter, telling him that his child's forehead feels hot and that she is complaining of not feeling well. Sitting in traffic, the parent remembers that he does not know the whereabouts of the digital thermometer, so he decides to stop and purchase one. The parking lot at the store is extremely busy, so the parent decides to park in a handicapped spot, even though he does not have any mobility challenges. These types of situations have been addressed by philosophers such as Immanuel Kant, who spoke of the **categorical imperative**, which he defined as, "Act only according to that maxim whereby you can, at the same time, will that it should become a universal law." In other words, one's action should be considered in light of what would happen if everyone were to engage in the same action. While it might not seem like a harmful infraction, if everyone were to do it, then it would cause a true inconvenience and possible suffering for mobility-impaired individuals, for whom those spaces were designated. A deontological ethical viewpoint would determine that it is always wrong to park in the handicapped space, regardless of the situation. In real life, it is very difficult to adopt a 100% deontological viewpoint for dispute resolution. Often, the reason the dispute has arisen in the first place is because of some ambiguity inherent in the situation. In these cases, mediators must apply their best judgment to help the disagreeing parties see one another's viewpoints and to guide them toward a mutually amicable solution.

Figure 2.4 Sometimes ethical issues have no clear-cut answers and mediators must rely upon their best judgement. (Credit: George Becker/ pexels/ License: CC0)

Future Directions in Mediation

As technology continues to change the ways we interact with one another, it is likely that we will see advances in mediation techniques. For example, there are companies that offer online mediation services, known as **e-mediation**. E-mediation can be useful in situations where the parties are geographically far apart, or the transaction in dispute took place online. Ebay uses e-mediation to handle the sheer volume of misunderstandings between parties. Research has shown that one of the benefits of e-mediation is that it allows people the time needed to "cool down" when they have to explain their feelings in an email, as opposed to speaking to others in person.

In addition to technological advancements, new findings in psychology are influencing how disputes are resolved, such as the rising interest in canine-assisted mediation (CAM), in which the presence of dogs is posited to have an impact on human emotional health. Since the presence of dogs has a positive impact on many of the neurophysiological stress markers in humans, researchers are beginning to explore the use of therapy animals to assist in dispute resolution.

Figure 2.5 Mediation experts are considering the benefits of therapy dogs for canine-assisted mediation. (Credit: Garfield Besa/ pexels/ License: CC0)

2.3 Arbitration

The American Bar Association (ABA) defines arbitration as the "private process where disputing parties agree that one or several individuals can make a decision about the dispute after receiving evidence and hearing arguments." Arbitration is overseen by a neutral **arbitrator**, or an individual who is responsible for making a decision on how to resolve a dispute and who has the ability to decide on an **award**, or a course of action that the arbiter believes is fair, given the situation. An award can be a monetary payment that one party must pay to the other; however, awards need not always be financial in nature. An award may require that one business stop engaging in a certain practice that is deemed unfair to the other business. As distinguished from mediation, in which the mediator simply serves as a facilitator who is attempting to help the disagreeing parties reach an agreement, and arbitrator acts more like a judge in a court trial and often has legal expertise, although he or she may or may not have subject matter expertise. Many arbitrators are current or retired lawyers and judges.

Types of Arbitration Agreements

Parties can enter into either voluntary or involuntary arbitration. In **voluntary arbitration**, the disputing parties have decided, of their own accord, to seek arbitration as a way to potentially settle their dispute. Depending on the state's laws and the nature of the dispute, disagreeing parties may have to attempt arbitration before resorting to litigation; this requirement is known as **involuntary arbitration** because it is forced upon them by an outside party.

Arbitration can be either binding or non-binding. In **binding arbitration**, the decision of the arbitrator(s) is final, and except in rare circumstances, neither party can appeal the decision through the court system. In **non-binding arbitration**, the arbitrator's award can be thought of as a recommendation; it is only finalized if both parties agree that it is an acceptable solution. This fact is why non-binding arbitration can be useful for what the American Arbitration Association describes as "disputes where the parties may be too far apart in their viewpoints to mediate or are in need of an objective evaluation of their respective positions." Having a neutral party assess the situation may help disputants to rethink and reassess their positions and reach a future compromise.

Issues Covered by Arbitration Agreements

There are many instances in which arbitration agreements may prove helpful as a form of alternative dispute resolution. While arbitration can be useful for resolving family law matters, such as divorce, custody, and child support issues, in the domain of business law, it has three major applications:

- **Labor**. Arbitration has often been used to resolve labor disputes through interest arbitration and grievance arbitration. **Interest arbitration** addresses disagreements about the terms to be included in a new contract, e.g., workers of a union want their break time increased from 15 to 25 minutes. In contrast, **grievance arbitration** covers disputes about the implementation of existing agreements. In the example previously given, if the workers felt they were being forced to work through their 15-minute break, they might engage in this type of arbitration to resolve the matter.
- **Business Transactions**. Whenever two parties conduct business transactions, there is potential for misunderstandings and mistakes. Both business-to-business transactions and business-to-consumer transactions can potentially be solved through arbitration. Any individual or business who is unhappy with a business transaction can attempt arbitration. Jessica Simpson recently won an arbitration case in which she disputed the release of a fitness video she had made because she felt the editor took too long to release it.
- **Property Disputes**. Business can have various types of property disputes. These might include disagreements over physical property, e.g., deciding where one property ends and another begins, or intellectual property, e.g., trade secrets, inventions, and artistic works.

Typically, civil disputes, as opposed to criminal matters, attempt to use arbitration as a means of dispute resolution. While definitions can vary between municipalities, states, and countries, a **civil matter** is generally one that is brought when on party has a grievance against another party and seeks monetary damages. In contrast, in a **criminal matter**, a government pursues an individual or group for violating laws meant to establish the best interests of the public. While the word **crime** often invokes the idea of violence, there are many crimes, such as embezzlement, in which the harm caused is not physical, but rather monetary.

Ethics of Commercial Arbitration Clauses

As previously discussed, going to court to solve a dispute is a costly endeavor, and for large companies, it is possible to incur millions of dollars in legal expenses. While arbitration is meant to be a form of dispute resolution that helps disagreeing parties find a low-cost, time-efficient solution, it has become increasingly important to question *whose* expenses are being lowered, and to what effect. Many consumer advocates are fighting against what are known as **forced-arbitration clauses**, in which consumers agree to settle all disputes through arbitration, effectively waiving their right to sue a company in court. Some of these forced arbitration clauses cause the other party to forfeit their right to appeal an arbitration decision or participate in any kind of **class action lawsuit**, in which individuals who have a similar issue sue as one collective group. For example, in 2006, Enron investors initiated a class action lawsuit against executives who hid the company's losses and were awarded $7.2 billion dollars. While this example represents a case where the company being sued was clearly in the wrong, it is important for large companies to be ethical in their use of arbitration clauses. They should not be used as a way to keep wrongdoings "quiet" or to limit consumers' abilities to obtain rightful retribution for products and services that do not perform as promised.

Arbitration Procedures

When parties enter into arbitration, certain procedures are followed. First, the number of arbitrators is decided, along with how they will be chosen. Parties that enter into willing arbitration may have more control over this decision, while those that do so unwillingly may have a limited pool of arbitrators from which to choose. In the case of willing arbitration, parties may decide to have three arbitrators, one chosen by each of the disputants and the third chosen by the elected arbitrators.

Next, a timeline is established, and evidence is presented by both parties. Since arbitration is less formal than court proceedings, the evidence phase typically goes faster than it would in a courtroom setting. Finally, the arbitrator will make a decision and usually makes one or more awards.

Not all arbitration agreements have the same procedures. It depends on the types of agreements made in advance by the disputing parties. Consider the following scenario: the owner of a large commercial office building uses a lease agreement, which stipulates that arbitration will be used to settle the renewal terms of a lease. For example, the lease may state that, at the end of year one, the second year's lease payment will be at current market value, and if the tenants cannot agree on that value, they will then allow an arbitrator to decide. If the building owner feels that the renewal rate should be $40/square foot and the tenant feels it should be $20/square foot, an arbiter who may not be an expert in local real estate values might decide to resolve the dispute by using a rule of thumb, such as "splitting the difference." In this case, the arbiter might decide that $30/square foot represents a fair lease renewal rate.

Figure 2.6 Various types of arbitration can be employed depending on what the parties think is best for their situation. (Credit: Tim Eiden/ pexels/ License: CC0)

To overcome this shortcoming, the building owner could write a lease agreement that stipulates that the parties use binding **baseball arbitration** and use subject matter experts as arbitrators. In this case, that might include real estate attorneys or commercial real estate investors. In baseball arbitration, each party would submit a lease renewal figure to an arbitrator. For example, imagine that the renewing tenant submits an offer of $10/per square foot, which is very much under market value, while the building owner submits an offer of $35/square foot. In this scenario, the arbitrator chooses one offer or the other, without modification. This type of arbitration incentivizes both parties to be fair in their dealings with one another because to do otherwise would be to their own detriment.

Arbitration Awards

An arbiter can issue either a "bare bones" or a reasoned award. A **bare bones** award refers to one in which the arbitrator simply states his or her decision, while a **reasoned** award lists the rationale behind the decision and award amount. The decision of the arbitrator is often converted to a judgement, or legal tool that allows the winning party to pursue collection action on the award. The process of converting an award to a judgement is known as confirmation.

Judicial Enforcement of Arbitration Awards

While it might seem that the party that is awarded a settlement by an arbitrator has reason to be relieved that the matter is resolved, sometimes this decision represents just one more step toward actually receiving the award. While a party may honor the award and voluntarily comply, this outcome is not always the case. In cases where the other party does not comply, the next step is to petition the court to enforce the arbitrator's decision. This task can be accomplished by numerous mechanisms, depending on the governing laws. These include writs of execution, garnishment, and liens.

- **Writ of Execution**. Cornell Law School defines a writ of execution as "A court order that directs law enforcement personnel to take action in an attempt to satisfy a judgment won by the plaintiff."
- **Garnishment**. A garnishment refers to a court order that seizes the money, typically wages, to satisfy a debt. A myriad of laws apply to wage garnishment, e.g., certain types of income, such as Social Security Disability Income (SSDI), cannot be garnished. In addition, depending on state laws, sometimes only debtors who make over a certain amount, e.g. $1,600 gross/month, are subject to wage garnishment.
- **Liens**. A lien gives the entitled party in a judgement the right to seize the property of another to satisfy a debt. Commonly, liens can be placed on real estate and personal property, such as automobiles and boats. Property that has a lien cannot be sold because the title is encumbered and often cannot be legally transferred until the lien is satisfied, or paid. Depending on state laws, only certain property is subject to a lien. For example, the winning party in an arbitration case may only be able to place a lien on the other party's vehicle if it has a market value of over $7,500.

The enforcement of arbitration awards is governed by a number of laws, such as Federal Arbitration Act and Uniform Arbitration Act.

Summary

Negotiation, mediation, and arbitration are alternatives form of dispute resolution that attempt to help disagreeing parties avoid the time and expense of court litigation. While negotiation is involved in all three forms, mediation and arbitration involve a neutral third party to help the parties find a solution. Frameworks that consider self-interest, as opposed to interest in the other party, can help negotiators craft successful negotiation approaches. Mediators, arbitrators, and groups of arbitrators all follow certain steps and play in important role in trying to help parties reach common ground and avoid court proceedings. Mediators who establish rapport with disputing parties can facilitate dispute resolution, as mediation is very much solution-focused. Arbitrators must often decide upon awards when parties cannot reach an agreement. Even when an aggrieved party attains an arbitration award, it may still have to pursue the other party by using a variety of legal techniques to enforce the payment or practice stipulated by the award. Staying current with federal and state laws associated with negotiation proceedings is essential for businesses looking to maximize their relational and outcome goals.

Assessment Questions

1. A process in which a third party selected by the disputants helps the parties to voluntarily resolve their disagreement is known as:

a. Mediation.
b. Discovery.
c. Arbitration.
d. Settlement.

2. What's the first step in Alternative Dispute Resolution?

a. Conciliation.
b. Mediation.
c. Negotiation.
d. Arbitration.

3. What's the definition of negotiation?

This OpenStax book is available for free at http://cnx.org/content/col30149/1.5

4. How does the process of negotiation work?

5. Explain the Thomas-Kilmann Conflict Mode Instrument.

6. A person trained in conflict resolution is considered:

a. An arbitrator.
b. A mediator.
c. A negotiator.
d. A judge.

7. Mediation focuses on:

a. Solutions.
b. Testimony.
c. Expert witnesses.
d. Discoveries.

8. Name the steps in Mediation.

9. What's the main benefit of e-mediation?

10. Roger and Larry are having a dispute regarding their joint business. They want to have a binding resolution to their dispute, but they would prefer to have the dispute handled privately and by someone with special expertise. The best form of dispute resolution for their problem would be:

a. Arbitration.
b. Litigation.
c. Mediation.
d. Summary Jury Trial.

11. All of the following are methods to enforce an arbitrator's decision except:

a. Writs of Execution.
b. Garnishment.
c. Fines.
d. Liens.

12. Describe the typical steps in Arbitration.

13. Explain the differences between binding and non-binding arbitration.

14. All of the following are the most common applications of arbitration in the business context except:

a. Labor.
b. Business Transactions.
c. Property Disputes.
d. Torts.

15. The following are the type of awards that may be issue by an arbitrator:

a. Bare Bones.
b. Reasoned.
c. Both a and b.
d. Neither a nor b.

Endnotes

He, L. (April 2013). Tim Cook's apology letter to Apple customer in China. Forbes. Retrieved from: https://www.forbes.com/sites/laurahe/2013/04/03/tim-cooks-apology-letter-to-customers-in-china/#510458b51ea3.

Kilmann, R. H., & Thomas, K. W. (1977). Developing a forced-choice measure of conflict-handling behavior: The "MODE" instrument. *Educational and psychological measurement*, 37(2), 309–325.

Top 10 International Business Negotiation Case Studies. Program on Negotiation. Harvard Law School. Retrieved from: https://www.pon.harvard.edu/daily/international-negotiation-daily/top-negotiation-case-studies-in-international-negotiations-from-business-and-global-politics/.

Pinkley, R. L., Neale, M. A., & Bennett, R. J. (1994). The impact of alternatives to settlement in dyadic negotiation. *Organizational Behavior and Human Decision Processes*, 57(1), 97–116.

Pruitt, D. G. (1983). Strategic choice in negotiation. *American Behavioral Scientist*, 27(2), 167–194.

Pruitt, D. G., & J. Z. Rubin. (1986). Social conflict: Escalation, stalemate, and settlement. New York: Random House.

Uniform Trusts Act. Cornell University Law School. Retrieved from: https://www.law.cornell.edu/uniform/vol7#arbit.

Carver, T., & Vondra, A. (May–June 1994). Alternative dispute resolution: Why it works and why it doesn't. Harvard Business Review. Retrieved from: https://hbr.org/1994/05/alternative-dispute-resolution-why-it-doesnt-work-and-why-it-does.

MacKinnon, D. P., Lockwood, C. M., Hoffman, J. M., West, S. G., & Sheets, V. (2002). A comparison of methods to test mediation and other intervening variable effects. *Psychological methods*, 7(1), 83.

McGuire, J. Twelve tips for launching a mediation practice. General Practice, Solo and Small Firm Division The American Bar Association. Retrieved from: https://www.americanbar.org/publications/gp_solo/2011/september/twelve_tips_launching_mediation_practice.html.

Mediation: the six stages. NOLO. Retrieved from: https://www.nolo.com/legal-encyclopedia/mediation-six-stages-30252.html.

Paul, D. *Canine-assisted mediation*. Retrieved from: http://www.hnlr.org/wp-content/uploads/HNLR-Paul-Final.pdf.

Using E-Mediation and Online Mediation Techniques for Conflict Resolution. Program on Negotiation. *Harvard Law School*. Retrieved from: https://www.pon.harvard.edu/daily/mediation/dispute-resolution-using-online-mediation/.

What makes a good mediator? Program on Negotiation. Harvard Law School. Retrieved from: https://www.pon.harvard.edu/daily/mediation/what-makes-a-good-mediator/.

Arbitration. American Bar Association. Retrieved from: https://www.americanbar.org/groups/dispute_resolution/resources/DisputeResolutionProcesses/arbitration.html.

Dunlap, K. (May 2010). Singer Jessica Simpsons wins arbitration case. FindLaw. Retrieved from: https://blogs.findlaw.com/celebrity_justice/2010/05/singer-jessica-simpson-wins-arbitration-case.html.

Elkouri, F., Elkouri, E. A., Ruben, A. M., American Bar Association, & Employment Law. (1985). *How arbitration works*. Washington, DC: Bureau of National Affairs.

Farber, H. S. (1981). Splitting-the-difference in interest arbitration. *ILR Review*, 35(1), 70–77.

Use 'Baseball Arbitration' to settle rent disputes at renewal time. Commercial Lease Law Insider. Retrieved from: https://www.stroock.com/siteFiles/Pub391.pdf.

What We Do (n.d.). American Arbitration Association. Retrieved from: https://www.adr.org/Arbitration.

Writ of Execution (n.d.). Cornell Law School. Retrieved from: https://www.law.cornell.edu/wex/writ_of_execution.

3 Business Ethics and Social Responsibility

Figure 3.1 (Credit: rawpixel/ pixabay/ Attribution 2.0 Generic (CC BY 2.0))

Chapter Outline

3.1 Business Ethics
3.2 Social Responsibility

Introduction

Learning Outcome

- Analyze the role of ethics and social responsibility in business.

3.1 Business Ethics

Businesses must establish a clear set of values that promote ethical practices and social responsibility. In today's business climate, companies are increasingly under scrutiny by private citizens. A company that builds its foundation on sound principles will have a better chance of staying competitive in a volatile market.

Figure 3.2 A group of employees who uphold strong corporate values can be an asset to the company they work for. (Credit: rawpixel/ pexels/ License: CC0)

Business ethics are considered to be the blueprint for building a successful organization. If an organization is built on socially responsible values, it will be stronger than an organization that is built on profit alone. More than just a positive reputation, the core ethics of a business dictate how every decision, process, and procedure will take place. This steadfast governance applies even if the business faces hard times or difficult situations. Some will even argue that businesses require full transparency in today's world.

Over the last few decades, numerous cases of bad business practices have made headlines. From McDonalds' funding of President Nixon's campaign in an effort to reduce workers' wages in the 1970s, to the more recent case of Uber employees alleging sexual harassment and the company's CEO having a public meltdown in the back of a driver's car, there's no shortage of ethics-related problems in the business world. Businesses are more than people working together to offer a product or service. Businesses are often viewed as entities that should protect stakeholders from unethical behaviors and activities. A set of governing rules should be in place to set the bar high for ethical compliance in every organization.

Why Is Corporate Ethics So Important in Business?

The idea of business ethics may seem subjective, but it comes down to acceptable levels of behavior for each individual who makes up the organization. This behavior must start at the top with responsible actions demonstrated by leadership. By doing so, leaders create a set of rules that are to be followed by others in the company. These rules can be based on the deep values that the company has concerning the quality of products and services, the commitment to customers, or how the organization gives something back to the community. The more a company lives by its set of ethics, the more likely it is to be successful.

Anna Spooner, who writes for LovetoKnow, shares tips on how to evaluate whether or not an organization is creating ethical practices by determining the impact of each practice. Some examples include:

Executive compensation rates during employee layoffs. Let's say a company is struggling during an economic downturn and must lay off a portion of its workforce. Does the CEO of the company take his or her annual raise or take a pay cut when others are losing their jobs? One could say that to take a raise is unethical because the CEO should also sacrifice some pay for the good of the company.

Fair compensation for employees. Paying employees minimum wage, or just above minimum wage, is not always fair compensation. In most regions, the cost of living has not been adjusted in years, meaning that people are surviving on less money. Ethics can make a difference here.

Ethical business practices, guided by a corporate set of standards, can have many positive outcomes, including recruitment and retention improvement, better relationships with customers, and positive PR. In 2015, Dan Price, CEO of the Seattle payment processing firm Gravity Payments, voluntarily took a huge pay cut and vowed to raise his employees' wages to $70,000. This move was great for the company, which claims that revenues and profits skyrocketed, and they experienced a 91 percent employee retention rate over the last few years.

On the opposite side, unethical business behaviors can have a negative impact on any business. Even if an unethical decision is made by a single member of the executive team, it can have far-reaching repercussions.

Some possible results of unethical business actions may include:

Poor company reputation. In an increasingly transparent world, unethical decisions made by businesspeople become permanent stains on the company. Social networks have become sounding boards for anything deemed unethical or politically incorrect, and everyone from disgruntled employees to dissatisfied customers can rate companies on public company review websites.

Negative employee relations. If employees continually see a discrepancy between what's expected of them and how leadership behaves, this contrast can create serious problems in the management of employees. Some employees may become disengaged, while others will stop working as hard. After all, if the same rules don't apply to everyone, why even bother? The downside to negative employee relations is that the entire company becomes less productive, less responsive to customers, and less profitable.

Recruitment and retention problems. Once a company has developed a negative reputation, it can be difficult to recruit new talent, let alone retain the talent that's already there. Disengaged employees who grow tired of the double standards will leave. This attrition can impact customers who then have to deal with less experienced and less interested employees, who are already overworked and frustrated.

Company credibility lost. Customers are savvy enough to follow what's going on from an ethics standpoint. If they hear of a problem, they begin to question the actions of every person at the company. For example, if a member of the board is accepting expensive gifts from clients in exchange for favorable pricing of materials, this situation could set off major alarms for other customers, and even vendors. The company can expect to lose business if this unethical behavior continues.

As you can see, poor ethics can quickly spiral downward, destroying every aspect of the business and making it very difficult to compete. It's critical for every business to pay attention to ethical standards and continually remind employees at all levels that their behavior has an impact on the entire organization.

History of Corporate Governance

The concept of corporate governance is relatively new compared to the entire history of free trade and business formation. There was likely some "code of honor" followed by businesses in the past, but it wasn't until the 21st century that greater attention was paid to how companies operate and how the operation impacts employees and the communities in which they serve.

According to the Ethics and Compliance Initiative, which is comprised of organizations that are committed to creating best practices in ethics, each decade has been influenced by external factors, such as war or economic turmoil, combined with major ethical focal areas, and the result has been the development of ethics and compliance programs. For example, in the mid-1980s, the United States was thrust into a recessionary period. During this period, government contractors were billing outrageous amounts for equipment and services, further increasing the government's deficit.

At the same time, larger companies began downsizing to cut costs, which eroded the trust that employees once had. People felt the need to look out for themselves. Greed appeared to be everywhere, from political bribes to the earliest financial schemers. As a result, General Dynamics established the first business ethics office in 1985 to crack down on this kind of activity, and other companies created ombudsman positions to help ethics officers identify and prosecute corporate ethics violators.

Ethical Decision-Making Policies

In any organization, sound moral, business, and financial practices must be followed at all times. No one is above the law or has special privileges when it comes to ethics. Decision making needs to happen with corporate governance in mind. According to Michigan State University, the six steps to ethical decision making are:

1. Make sure leaders understand the issue at hand and have gathered all of the facts related to it.
2. Leaders should list all of the facts they know, and list any assumptions they are making about the issue. This step ensures that the leaders keep the facts and assumptions differentiated and in mind.
3. Note all of the concerns related to the issue, including all of the people concerned, the laws related to the issue, and any corporate or professional ethical guidelines that may be involved.
4. Construct a potential solution to the problem.
5. Evaluate the proposed solution, making sure to consider all of the ethical aspects noted in step 3.
6. Once leaders have come to a solution, they recommend it, as well as any actions that need to be taken.

Establishing a Code of Conduct

To educate and guide others in the organization, a set of ethics, or a code of conduct, should be developed and distributed. Kimberlee Leonard, who writes for the **Houston Chronicle**, states, "A code of ethics is important for businesses to establish to ensure that everyone in the company is clear on the mission, values and guiding principles of the company." While it takes some time to create a code of conduct, the ideals involved should already be present in the company's culture.

The elements that belong in a code of conduct, according to Kimberlee Leonard, are:

Legal considerations. The business is a legal entity, and therefore all employees should be thinking about their behavior and how it could easily turn into a lawsuit. Establishing conduct rules at this level can clear up any gray areas. For example, a company should define what sexual harassment is and what to do if an employee experiences it. New items that detail specific codes of conduct can be added as they come up.

Value-based ethics. These are specific ethics that dig under the surface of a corporate culture. A business should think about how it wants to be viewed by the community. Examples could be a commitment to green office practices, reduction of a company's carbon footprint, giving a certain percentage of a company's profits to the local food pantry to support the community, etc.

Regulatory ethics. These are designed to maintain certain standards of performance based on the industry. One example is a commitment to maintaining data privacy at all times, as it pertains to customer records. This element defines how employees are to handle sensitive data and what will happen if someone doesn't follow the rules.

Professional behaviors. One should never assume that just because someone puts on a business suit and goes to work that he or she will behave professionally. Problems such as bullying, harassment, and abuse can happen in the workplace. Establishing behavioral standards for professionalism should include what is acceptable in the office, while traveling, during meetings, and after hours, when colleagues meet with clients and one another.

A good code of conduct is a working document that can be updated and shared as needed. Many companies include this document as part of their employee manual, while others use a secure intranet for displaying this information. No matter where it is housed, employees need to be educated on the code of conduct and refer to it often, starting on the first day on the job.

What to Do When Something Goes Wrong

It should be noted that along with a code of conduct, there needs to be a clear "whistleblower" policy in which violators are identified and action is taken. This process should be handled with complete confidentiality and sensitivity to the company and all parties involved. Retaliation should never be tolerated when it comes to ethics violations. The company should have a step-by-step plan of action for dealing with ethics problems at all levels, up to and including the executive leadership of the company. A third-party investigative firm can be used to handle such matters to remove the burden and influence that internal resources may have.

3.2 Social Responsibility

Over the last few decades, there has been a movement throughout the global business community to improve the world through smarter use of resources and giving back to communities. This movement is called corporate social responsibility. The concept is catching on at companies that range in size from small startups to large Fortune 500 corporations. In the following section, you will learn what social responsibility is and how it is a win-win for businesses and consumers.

Figure 3.3 Employees often like to participate in volunteer activities through their employer. (Credit: rawpixel/ pixabay/ License: CC0)

What Is Corporate Responsibility?

Corporate responsibility refers to the idea that a business is given the opportunity and privilege to make the world a better place. This process can happen through a variety of methods, including the donation of funds, volunteerism, and implementation of environmentally friendly policies. It is up to each organization to determine the best way to demonstrate social responsibility.

While certainly not mandatory, corporate social responsibility has become a popular way for companies to improve their image and promote causes they believe in at the same time. Corporate social responsibility may involve focusing on the immediate community in which a company does business. However, there are some organizations that take it a step further and focus on more widespread global issues. For example, the shoe company TOMS has created a mission to make sure that every boy and girl in underprivileged countries has proper footwear. Blake Mycoskie, CEO of TOMS, has created a complete business model around social responsibility. Not stopping at shoes, the company now also helps with bringing fresh water to communities, as well as making birth safer for babies in developing nations.

The popularity of corporate social responsibility has only increased as millennials and Generation Z employees enter the workforce. Employees in these generations often care deeply about making a difference in the world in which they work. Whether they are buying products from brands that give back or promoting a similar activity in their own place of employment, the youngest of the workforce are making corporate social responsibility a priority.

Where Did the Concept Originate?

Corporate social responsibility is not a new construct. One could go back hundreds of years and find examples of corporate philanthropy and social support. However, the earliest published book about the topic is

Corporate Responsibility of the Businessman, published in 1953. This book introduced the concept of companies giving back as a form of investment in the future. This idea came from a generation that had survived some of the hardest times in our world and wanted to make it a better place for generations to come.

By the turn of the millennium, companies were actively participating in a variety of corporate social responsibility projects, from volunteerism to large corporate-matched charitable donations. Nearly every company has some form of charitable campaign, driven by the values of the culture and the interests of employees. Today, some 63 million Americans volunteer each year, which is worth around $175 billion in worker hours annually (Source: Corporation for National and Community Service). On top of volunteering, U.S. corporations give over $18 billion to charities each year through fundraisers and employee-employer matching programs (Source: Giving USA).

How Does Corporate Responsibility Benefit a Business?

There are many ways that corporate social responsibility can benefit a business and its objectives. Aside from being able to promote the causes that are closely connected to the values of the company, a business can improve its reputation exponentially.

Benefits of corporate social responsibility include many direct and indirect effects. Based on research from the Kellogg School of Management at Northwestern University, these can include:

Improved perception by investors. If a company reports corporate social responsibility spending that exceeds the expectations of investors, this dollar amount is a sign that the company itself is in good financial standing. This perception results in positive stock returns and increased confidence by investors.

Enhanced performance for going green. Researchers have found that when companies focus on eco-friendly efforts, the positive impact on operational performance heading into the second year is remarkable. Those that expand their efforts in more complex ways and in collaboration with industry standard-setting associations (such as LEED), or other eco-friendly companies, increase their performance even more.

Contracting for success. In companies that tie their CEO's salary to corporate social responsibility results, also known as contracting, the impact is felt even more. The value of the company increases while the bottom line of the business is maintained.

The benevolent halo effect. When consumers understand the commitment that an organization has to being socially responsible, its image becomes more positive. Customers actually perceive the company and its products in a different way because they expect a better experience.

Consistency of efforts and partnerships. Researchers also found that socially responsible organizations were consistent with staying focused on the issues that mattered most to their employees and customers. A higher level of consistency of efforts prompted better results.

There are some other benefits of being a socially responsible company. These may happen as a result of internal factors, as well as how closely matched the efforts are to the culture. Alison Robins, writer for OfficeVibe, explains that being socially responsible can help attract positive attention from outside of a company. Some examples include:

Talent attraction. Many companies offer employees paid time off to participate in volunteer activities, including travel to other nations. Who wouldn't want to work for a company that cares so much about a personal cause? Corporate social responsibility is often used as a recruitment tool to attract people who care about giving back to their communities and making changes that impact the world.

Consumer influence. A major benefit of engaging in corporate social responsibility efforts is that consumers regularly check in with their favorite brands to see what they are doing, and they are influenced to make purchases so they can be part of this community. With the process of posting messages on social networks, entire movements can take off via the support of loyal consumers.

Promoting Corporate Responsibility with Marketing

After reviewing the benefits of corporate social responsibility and some of the examples provided by popular companies, it is easy to see how important proper marketing can be to to this effort. As you can see from the following example of Tom's One for One™ program, marketing is used as a reminder for consumers that the company is committed to providing one pair of shoes to a child in an undeveloped nation for every pair purchased by a consumer.

Marketing is powerful in terms of the consumer market. It has been estimated by the brand marketing news source *Adweek* that millennials represent around $2.45 trillion in spending per year. Cone Communications, a public relations and marketing agency, found that 60 percent more millennials will engage with brands that discuss and market to social issues. Younger consumers are attracted to brands that authentically market their products alongside social responsibility campaigns.

However, one should not use corporate social responsibility as a marketing pitch for a company. Consumers will quickly pick up on this tactic, and it can damage the brand. Nicole Fallon, who contributes to *Business News Daily*, reveals, "The motivation behind many companies' CSR efforts actually provides the very reason that they shouldn't take on socially responsible initiatives." Motivations such as competitive positioning and profitability are not authentic when it comes to corporate social responsibility.

It is also important to distinguish between corporate social responsibility and social marketing. Often used interchangeably, there are some key differences. Social marketing attempts to change the attitudes and behaviors of consumers by using a variety of marketing methods. However, corporate social responsibility is a sustainable effort that can be measured. Bernard Okhakume, a brand management consultant, advised *Daily Times*, "For a corporate social responsibility project to be successful, several factors come into play: the project needs to be sustainable, its topic and practice abide by ethical standards, sensitive to society's needs, embraced and supported by the company's employees, create the aimed effect on the target audience, and every year, and the project needs to be evaluated to see how beneficial it is."

The Financial Impact of the Triple Bottom Line

When examining the value of corporate responsibility, one must understand the concept of the triple bottom line (TBL), which essentially measures the sustainability of an organization's social responsibility efforts. The term includes three dimensions of a giving business—profits, people, and the planet. Without one of these factors, there cannot be a balance. According to economist Andrew Savitz, the triple bottom line "captures the essence of sustainability by measuring the impact of an organization's activities on the world ... including both its profitability and shareholder values and its social, human and environmental capital."

The challenge with the TBL model is that while profits can be measured in dollars, and people can be measured in numbers, it can be difficult to measure the impact of social responsibility. Some argue that this task is dependent upon what is being measured. For example, if one is saving the rainforest, a reasonable unit of measurement could be acreage. Progress toward protecting this resource could be recorded as how many fewer acres have been forested and how many native (people) communities have been saved as a result of the intervention.

Another example could be a social cause, such as creating housing for single parents in poverty-stricken neighborhoods in a specific city. The impact can be felt in terms of the additional housing that is created (built or rehabbed from existing homes), and the value that this effort brings to the neighborhood. The number of people helped can be measured. The city's rate of homelessness can be measured as it is reduced. Then, there are other equally important results of social responsibility that can be considered, such as the reduced rate of crime in areas with homeowners, and an increase in employment for those who own the homes. These indirect benefits have an impact on the company because it can eventually hire people from these areas of the city.

Businesses must be continually mindful of the image that they project to the world and be sure to align their corporate social responsibility campaigns with their culture. An authentic cause that is backed by all is far better than one that is dreamt up purely for the sake of marketing.

Assessment Questions

1. Define business ethics.

2. Who decides the business ethics for a company?

a. The HR department.
b. The employees.
c. Leadership.
d. Consultants.

3. All of the following are examples of results of unethical business actions except:

a. Recruitment and retention problems.
b. Lower employee salaries.
c. Negative employee relations.
d. Poor company reputation.

4. Ethical rules can be based on deep values of an organization which may include:

a. Quality of products and services.
b. Commitment to customers.
c. How the organization gives back to the community.
d. All of the above.

5. According to Kimberlee Leonard of the Houston Chronicle the elements that belong in a Code of Conduct for a company include all of the following except:

a. Office Hours.
b. Professional behaviors.
c. Regulatory ethics.
d. Legal considerations.

6. What's the definition of Corporate Responsibility?

7. Where did the term Corporate Responsibility originate?

8. The benefits of Corporate Responsibility for a business include:

a. Talent attraction.
b. Consumer influence.
c. Improved perception by investors.
d. All of the above.

9. The three dimensions of the triple bottom line include all of the following except:

a. Profits.
b. People.
c. Planet.
d. Promotion.

10. Distinguish between corporate social responsibility and social marketing.

Endnotes

Bisk. "6-Step Guide to Ethical Decision-Making" Michigan State University. Retrieved from: https://www.michiganstateuniversityonline.com/resources/leadership/guide-to-ethical-decision-making/#.W7KAq2hKiUI.

Ethics and Compliance Initiative. "Business Ethics and Compliance Timeline." Retrieved from: https://www.ethics.org/resources/free-toolkit/ethics-timeline/.

Georgescu, Peter. "What Are We Waiting For?" *Forbes*. Retrieved from: https://www.forbes.com/sites/petergeorgescu/2018/01/24/what-are-we-waiting-for/#6f5caff856e3.

Isidore, Chris. "Gravity Payments CEO takes 90% pay cut to give workers huge raise." *CNN Money*. Retrieved from: https://money.cnn.com/2015/04/14/news/companies/ceo-pay-cuts-pay-increases/index.html.

Leonard, Kimberlee. "Importance of Creating a Code of Ethics for a Business." *Chron Small Business*. Retrieved from: https://smallbusiness.chron.com/importance-creating-code-ethics-business-3094.html.

Nayab, N. "Real-World Examples of Bad Business Ethics." *Bright Hub*. Retrieved from: https://www.brighthub.com/office/entrepreneurs/articles/115557.aspx.

Shen, Linda. "The 10 Biggest Business Scandals of 2017." *Fortune*. Retrieved from: http://fortune.com/2017/12/31/biggest-corporate-scandals-misconduct-2017-pr/.

Spooner, A. "Importance of Ethics in Business." Love to Know. Retrieved from: https://business.lovetoknow.com/business-operations-corporate-management/importance-ethics-business.

"About Tom's" Retrieved from: https://www.toms.com/corporate-responsibility/.

Ames, Eden. "Millennial Demand for Corporate Social Responsibility Drives Change in Brand Strategies." American Marketing Association. Retrieved from: https://www.ama.org/publications/MarketingNews/Pages/millennial-demand-for-social-responsibility-changes-brand-strategies.aspx.

Anyebe, Godwin. "Between Corporate Social Responsibility and Social Marketing." *The Daily Times*. Retrieved from: https://dailytimes.ng/corporate-social-responsibility-social-marketing/.

Carroll, Archie B. "Corporate Social Responsibility." Research Gate. Retrieved from: https://www.researchgate.net/publication/273399199_Corporate_Social_Responsibility.

Corporation for National and Community Service. "Volunteering and Civic Life in America." Retrieved from:

ttps://www.nationalservice.gov/vcla.

Fallon, Nicole. "Why You Shouldn't Jump on the CSR Bandwagon." *Business News Daily*. Retrieved from: https://www.businessnewsdaily.com/6475-csr-brand-authenticity.html.

Lilly Family School of Philanthropy. "Giving USA 2015 Highlights." Retrieved from: https://doublethedonation.com/forms/documents/charitable-giving-report-giving-usa-2015.pdf.

Robins, Alison. "5 Benefits of Having a Socially Responsible Company." *Office Vibe*. Retrieved from: https://www.officevibe.com/blog/socially-responsible-companies.

Slaper, Timothy F., and Hall, Tanya J. "The Triple Bottom Line: What Is It and How Does It Work?" *Indiana Business Review.* Retrieved from: http://www.ibrc.indiana.edu/ibr/2011/spring/article2.html.

Stone, Emily. "Take 5: How Companies Benefit from Corporate Social Responsibility." *Kellogg Insight*. Retrieved from: https://insight.kellogg.northwestern.edu/article/benefits-of-corporate-social-responsibility.

4 Business and the United States Constitution

Figure 4.1 (Credit: geralt/ pixabay/ Attribution 2.0 Generic (CC BY 2.0))

Chapter Outline

4.1 Commerce Clause

4.2 Constitutional Protections

Introduction

Learning Outcome

- Explain the impact of the U.S. Constitution on business.

4.1 Commerce Clause

Figure 4.2 The United States Constitution is the supreme law of the land. (Credit: 1778011/ pixabay/ License: CC0)

The Constitution and the Law

Federal and state constitutions are a major source of business law. The **United States Constitution** is the supreme law of the United States. In addition to the individual constitutions established in each state, the U.S. Constitution sets out the fundamental rules and principles by which the country and individual states are governed. Constitutional law is the term used to describe the powers and limits of the federal and state governments as established in the Constitution. The political system that divides authority to govern between the state and federal governments is known as **federalism**, and this too is established in the Constitution. The Tenth Amendment states that any area over which the federal government is not granted authority through the Constitution is reserved for the state. This statement means that any federal legislation impacting business and commerce must be established by an expressed constitutional **grant of authority**.

Federal Preemption

The Founding Fathers created a federal system that would, at times, "preempt" state law through the **supremacy clause**, outlined in Article VI of the Constitution. In other words, since the U.S. Constitution is the "supreme law of the land," if a state law conflicts with the U.S. Constitution, the state law is declared invalid. When the federal constitutional law prevails over the state law, it is said that the state law has been **preempted**. Before that determination is made, the courts try to determine if Congress intended to preempt state law in enacting the particular provision in question. If the answer is "no," then those who are asserting protections of state law may make claims under state law. If the answer is "yes," however, federal law prevails.

The Tenth Amendment to the Constitution gives the states powers over areas of law not held exclusively by the federal government through the U.S. Constitution, e.g., states can make laws about how to get married, who may get married, or how to dissolve a marriage, as well as which activities are crimes and how the crimes will be punished. If the U.S. Constitution does give the federal government some power, however, then the federal government may exercise it, free from state interference. For instance, the U.S. Congress (the legislative branch of the federal government) has the power, among other things, to coin money, to create a military, to establish post offices, and to declare war. Since there is specific mention of these powers, states may not create their own currency, military, or postal service, and they may not declare war.

The Commerce Clause and The Affordable Care Act

After much debate, negotiation, and political wrangling, Congress passed the Patient Protection and Affordable Care Act (PPACA) in 2010, which was designed to increase the number of Americans who had access to health insurance (a policy initiative known as Obamacare). The Act included a provision mandating that individuals not insured through employment or who were otherwise exempt from receiving health insurance obtain minimum essential health insurance or face a penalty issued through the Internal Revenue Service (IRS). The National Federation of Independent Business (NFIB), supported by 26 of the 50 states, challenged the constitutionality of this particular provision, known as the individual mandate. Their argument was upheld by the 11th Circuit Court of Appeals, which ruled that Congress did not have the authority to enact this provision. Later, however, the appellate court determined that the individual mandate was severable from the remainder of the PPACA, so ultimately the Act was upheld.

The main source of authority for the federal regulation of interstate and international commerce is the **commerce clause**. This clause is established in Article I, Section 8, of the Constitution. The Article grants Congress the power to "regulate Commerce with foreign Nations, and among the several States, and with the Indian Tribes." Thus, the commerce clause serves to simultaneously empower the federal government, while

This OpenStax book is available for free at http://cnx.org/content/col30149/1.5

limiting state power.

So long as a federal regulation impacts interstate commerce, that regulation can be described as constitutional, according to the commerce clause. However, since the Constitution was first written, there have often been occasions when the judiciary system has needed to step in to interpret the meaning and implications of the commerce clause. In particular, there have been disputes over the intended meaning of the phrase "among the several States." Up until the 1930s, this phrase was interpreted in a literal way, so that activities subject to federal regulation were required to involve trade between the states. This strict interpretation actually served to limit the federal regulation of commerce.

The turning point in the interpretation of the commerce clause came with the 1937 case, NLRB v. Jones & Laughlin Steel Corp. The previous year, in the Carter v. Carter Coal Co case, the court invalidated a program, initiated under the New Deal, that had tried to regulate the labor practices of coal firms on the basis that these practices were local, and therefore had only an indirect impact on interstate commerce. In NLRB v. Jones & Laughlin Steel Corp, the court deviated from that decision by ruling that Congress could regulate employment practices at a steel plant because any stoppages at that plant would have a serious, detrimental impact on interstate commerce. The court concluded that since the steel industry is a networked industry that incorporates mines, plants, and factories from Minnesota to Pennsylvania, the manufacturing of steel properly falls under the jurisdiction of the commerce clause. In summing up, the court concluded that:

EXAMPLE 4.1

"Although activities may be intrastate in character when separately considered, if they have such a close and substantial relationship to interstate commerce that their control is essential or appropriate to protect that commerce from burdens or obstructions, Congress cannot be denied the power to exercise that control" (NLRB v. Jones & Laughlin Steel Corp., 301 U.S. 1 1937).

Challenges to and Reinterpretations of the Commerce Clause

Ever since the NLRB v. Jones & Laughlin Steel Corp case, Congress has invoked the commerce clause to rule on a diverse range of business and commercial activities, as well as to support social reforms that indirectly impact state commerce. Examination of the United States Code reveals that there are more than 700 legislative provisions that explicitly refer to foreign or interstate commerce. What is perhaps most remarkable is the sheer diversity of statutory areas covered by the commerce clause. Areas covered include the regulation of sporting activities, endangered species, energy regulation, gambling, firearms control, and even terrorism.

Examples of Federal Legislation Passed by Invoking the Commerce Clause

- The Controlled Substances Act
- The Federal Mine Safety and Health Act
- The Civil Rights Act
- Americans with Disabilities Act
- The Indian Child Welfare Act

While businesses have often challenged these statutes as existing outside of the realm of congressional authority, in most cases, the courts have upheld the statutes as being valid exercises of congressional power in line with the commerce clause. An exception is the 1995 case, United States v. Lopez. The case centered around the legality of the Gun-Free School Zone Act, which was a federal law that outlawed the possession of guns within 1,000 feet of a school. In a landmark case, the Court ruled that the Act was outside the scope of the commerce clause, and that Congress did not have the authority to regulate in an area that had "nothing to do with commerce, or any sort of enterprise."

A recent controversy pertaining to the commerce clause relates to the passing of the Affordable Care Act, as described earlier. Protestors claimed that the individual mandate aspect of the ACA should be treated as a regulation that affects interstate commerce. According to their argument, after the Act was implemented, there would be an increase in the sale and purchase of health care insurance, such that the market for health care should be seen as being significantly impacted by the Act. However, the Chief Justice of the Supreme Court, Justice Roberts, ruled that actions that create new business activity do not affect interstate commerce.

Police Power and the Dormant Commerce Clause

The authority of the federal government to regulate interstate commerce has, at times, come into conflict with state authority over the same area of regulation. The courts have tried to resolve these conflicts with reference to the **police power** of the states.

Police power refers to the residual powers granted to each state to safeguard the welfare of their inhabitants. Examples of areas in which states tend to exercise their police power are zoning regulations, building codes, and sanitation standards for eating places. However, there are times when the states' use of police power impacts interstate commerce. If the exercise of the power interferes with, or discriminates against, interstate commerce, then the action is generally deemed to be unconstitutional. The limitation on the authority of states to regulate in areas that impact interstate commerce is known as the **dormant commerce clause**.

In using the dormant commerce clause to resolve conflicts between state and federal authority, the courts consider the extent to which the state law has a legitimate purpose. If it is determined that the state law has a legitimate purpose, then the court tries to determine whether the impact on interstate commerce is in the interest of the citizens of the state, and will rule accordingly. For instance, an ordinance that banned spray paint, issued in the city of Chicago, was challenged by paint manufacturers under the dormant commerce clause, but was ultimately upheld by the U.S. Court of Appeals because the ban was intended to reduce graffiti and related crimes.

Today, Congress uses its authority to regulate commercial activity in four general areas relating to the commerce clause:

1. Regulation of the channels of interstate commerce
2. Regulation of the instrumentalities of interstate commerce
3. Regulation of intangibles and tangibles that cross state lines
4. Regulation of activities that are deemed to be both economic and to have a substantial impact on interstate commerce

Area of Regulation	Explanation	Examples

Table 4.1

Regulation of the **channels** of interstate commerce	Channels of interstate commerce describe the passages of transportation between the states. Thus, the commerce clause authorizes Congress to regulate activities pertaining to the nation's airways, waterways, and roadways, and even where the activity itself takes place entirely in a single state.	For example, Congress can pass regulations that restrict what can be carried on airlines or on ships.
Regulation of the **instrumentalities** of interstate commerce	Instrumentalities of commerce are understood to be any resource employed in the carrying out of commerce. Examples of these resources are machines, equipment, vehicles, and personnel. Thus, Congress has the power to regulate these areas.	Congress could pass regulations mandating certain safety standards for equipment used in manufacturing plants.
Regulation of intangibles and tangibles that **cross state lines**	Any object, tangible or intangible, that crosses state lines can be regulated under the commerce clause. Tangible objects include goods purchased by consumers, as well as raw materials and equipment used in the production of goods for sale. Intangible objects include services, as well as electronic databases.	The Driver's Privacy Protection Act (DPPA) regulates the sale of information contained in the Department of Motor Vehicles' (DMV's) records.
Regulation of activities that are deemed to have a **substantial impact** on interstate commerce	Federal regulation of economic commercial activity expected to have a significant (as opposed to minor) effect on interstate commerce is constitutional, according to the commerce clause. Noneconomic commercial activity is not covered.	The courts in the United States vs. Lopez case described earlier deemed the Act to be unconstitutional because its terms have "nothing to do with 'commerce' or any sort of economic enterprise."

Table 4.1

4.2 Constitutional Protections

The Bill of Rights is the common term given to the first 10 amendments to the U.S. Constitution. These are not the only set of amendments to the Constitution, but they are considered together as impacting rights because they limit the ability of the federal government to infringe upon individual freedoms. In addition, a later amendment, the Fourteenth Amendment, extends the provisions set out in the Bill of Rights to the states, in addition to federal government. The Bill of Rights has a substantial impact upon government regulation of commercial activity, and therefore, it is important to fully understand it.

A summary of the provisions of the Bill of Rights is supplied below:

Amendment	Provision
First	Ensures that U.S. citizens have the right to freedom of speech, press, religion, and peaceable assembly. Provides citizens with the right to appeal to government to redress grievances.
Second	Establishes that the government cannot infringe upon citizens' right to bear arms. Establishes the importance of a militia for national security.
Third	Establishes that the government cannot quarter soldiers in private houses during peacetime or wartime.
Fourth	States that government can only issue warrants with probable cause and protects U.S. citizens from unwarranted search and seizure.
Fifth	Establishes rights of due process. Ensures that indictment of a grand jury is necessary to put a citizen on trial and grants citizens the right not to testify against themselves.
Sixth	Provides citizens with the right to an expeditious public trial, the right to an attorney, and the right to an impartial jury.
Seventh	States that citizens have the right to a trial by jury for common lawsuits involving monetary value of $20.
Eighth	Prohibits cruel and unusual punishment, prevents the imposition of excessive fines, and states that the government cannot set bail at excessive amounts.
Ninth	States that the rights set out in the Bill of Rights do not remove any other rights granted to citizens.
Tenth	States that any area over which the federal government is not granted authority through the Constitution is reserved for the states.

Table 4.2

Application of the Bill of Rights to Commercial Activity

The protections afforded the citizenry in the Bill of Rights are also extended to corporations and commercial activities. In the next sections, some applications of the various amendments in the area of business are discussed.

The First Amendment

The freedom of speech provisions in the First Amendment have application to corporations. The courts distinguish between different types of speech, and each has implications for the power of the federal government and states to regulate in these areas:

1. **Corporate Political Speech.** Political speech is any speech used to support political agendas or candidates. Until the 1970s, several states prevented firms from financially supporting political advertising because they feared the power of corporate assets. However, since the 1978 case **First National Bank of**

Boston v. Bellotti, it has been established that corporate political speech is protected in the same way as citizens' free speech.

2. **Unprotected Speech.** The 1942 case **Chaplinsky v. New Hampshire** determined that certain types of speech—that which could "inflict injury or incite an immediate breach of the peace"—is not protected under the First Amendment. Therefore, obscenities, defamation, and slanderous speech are not protected.
3. **Commercial Speech.** This type of speech conveys information pertaining to the sale of goods and services. Ever since the 1980 case **Hudson Gas & Electric Corp v. Public Service Commission of New York**, a four-part test has been established to determine whether commercial speech should be regulated according to the First Amendment. This test is known as The **Central Hudson Test for Commercial Speech.**

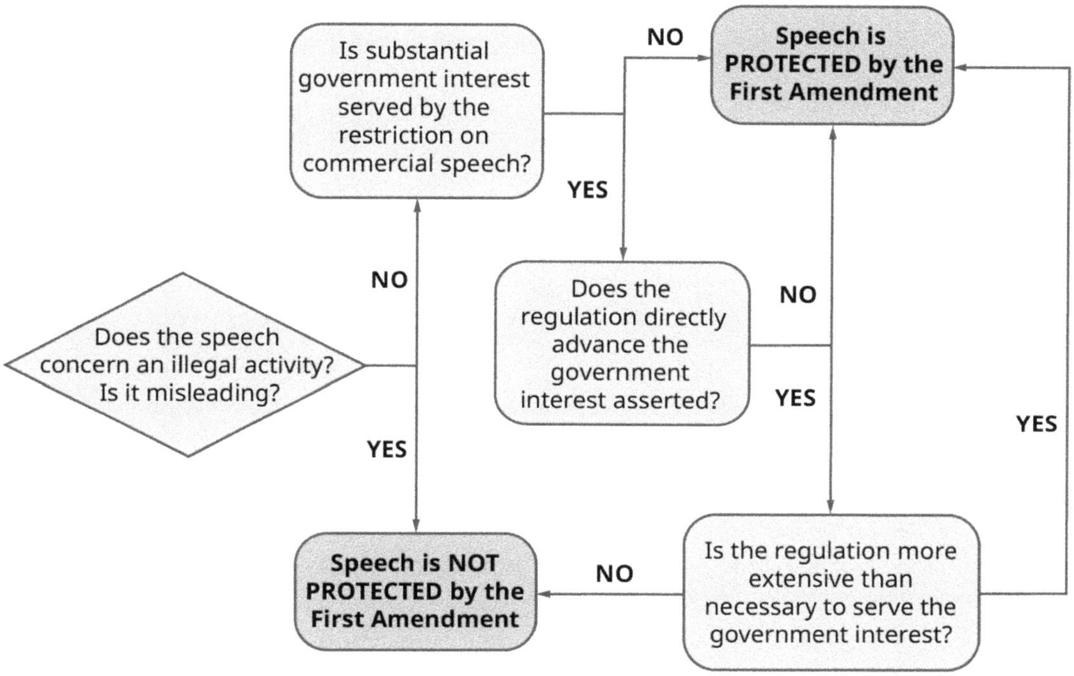

Figure 4.3 Hudson Gas & Electric Corp v. Public Service Commission of New York established a four-part test to determine whether commercial speech should be regulated according to the First Amendment. (Modification of art by BNED/pixabay Credit: CC BY NC SA)

The **free exercise clause** of the First Amendment states that government is prohibited from making laws that prohibit the free exercise of religion. Issues pertaining to this clause often arise in organizational settings. For example, historically, there have been a number of cases in which government employees have challenged employers' attempts to inhibit their exercise of religious practice (e.g., the wearing of religious symbols) in the workplace.

The Fourth Amendment

The Fourth Amendment guarantees that citizens are free from unreasonable searches and seizures, and requires government officials to obtain **search warrants** to conduct searches. However, government officials can only request a search warrant if they have **probable cause** to believe that criminal activity is occurring at the location of the search, or that they will locate evidence of criminal activity during the search (except where the official believes items will be removed prior to obtaining a warrant). The Fourth Amendment protects individual organizations and places of business, as well as residences. However, under the terms of the **pervasive-regulation exception,** administrative agencies can conduct warrantless searches of businesses attached to industries that have a long history of pervasive regulation. For example, public health agencies are allowed to conduct warrantless searches of stone quarries, as authorized by the Federal Mine Safety and Health Act of 1977.

The Fifth Amendment

For commercial enterprises and businesspeople, it is the **due process clause** of the Fifth Amendment that offers the most extensive protection. The clause states that the government cannot take an individual's life, liberty, or property without due process of law. Specifically, there are two types of due process:

- **Substantive due process** means that laws that will deprive an individual of his or her life, liberty, or property must be fair and not arbitrary. Laws passed should not affect fundamental rights, and regulations are required to meet the **rational-basis test.** In other words, the government must demonstrate that the law bears a rational relationship to a legitimate state interest. Many regulations affecting commercial activity, such as banking regulations, minimum wage laws, and regulations inhibiting unfair trade, have been tested against the rational-basis test.
- **Procedural due process** means that governments must use fair procedures when depriving an individual of his or her life, liberty, or property. This status quo does not only apply to federal criminal proceedings. For example, if a government employer discharges an employee from his job, or if the government suspends the driver's license of a worker, the employer must follow procedural due process.

Another clause contained in the Fifth Amendment that is relevant to commercial enterprises is the **takings clause.** According to this clause, when the government seizes private property for public use, it is required that the government pay the owner **just compensation** for the property. Just compensation is understood to be equivalent to the market value of the property. This clause has been broadly interpreted. For example, if environmental or safety regulations significantly impact the way in which a property owner can use his or her land for economic gain, the regulation can essentially be deemed as depriving the owner of his or her land, and the owner is entitled to compensation.

It is important to note that the **privilege against self-incrimination**, established under the Fifth Amendment (usually interpreted as the right to remain silent), only applies to sole proprietorships that are not legally distinct from the individual who owns them. Custodians and agents of corporations do not enjoy this privilege.

This OpenStax book is available for free at http://cnx.org/content/col30149/1.5

Figure 4.4 The various protections afforded the citizenry in the Bill of Rights are also extended to corporations and commercial activities. (Credit: Anthony Garand/ unsplash/ License: Unsplash License)

Assessment Questions

1. Explain Police Power and the Dormant Commerce Clause.

2. The Patient Protection and Affordable Care Act's (also known as Obamacare) provision that mandated that individuals not insured through employment obtain minimum essential health insurance or face a penalty was upheld as constitutional by the 11th Circuit.

a. True.
b. False.

3. The ____ gives the federal government the authority to regulate interstate and international commerce.

a. Supremacy Clause.
b. 10th Amendment.
c. Bill of Rights.
d. Commerce Clause.

4. The doctrine aimed at dividing the governing powers between the federal governments and the states is:

a. Judicial review.
b. Federalism.
c. Separation of powers.
d. Preemption.

5. The doctrine aimed at dividing the governing powers between the federal governments and the states is:

a. Commerce Clause.
b. Superior Clause.
c. Supremacy Clause.
d. Necessary and Proper Clause.

6. Describe the 2 types of Due Process.

7. The ____ of the constitution offers the most extensive protection for businesses.

a. Supremacy Clause.
b. Equal Protection Clause.
c. Due Process Clause.
d. Freedom of Speech Clause.

8. The 14th Amendment is a part of the Bill of Rights.

a. True.
b. False.

9. Which of the following is correct with regards to the powers of state government in the United States?

a. All powers not specifically enumerated to the federal government are reserved to the states.
b. The power over crimes is reserved to the federal government.
c. The power over the militia is reserved to the states.
d. The powers over the federal government are superior to every state power.

10. All of the sections of the Bill of Rights apply to corporations and commercial activities.

a. True.
b. False.

Endnotes

Beatty, J. F., Samuelson, S. S., & Abril, P. S. (2018). *Business law and the legal environment*. Cengage Learning.

Driesen, D. M. (2016). The economic/noneconomic activity distinction under the commerce clause. *Case W. Res. L. Rev.*, 67, 337.

United States v. Lopez, 514 U.S. 549, 558–559 (1995).

Beatty, J. F., Samuelson, S. S., & Abril, P. S. (2018). *Business law and the legal environment*. Cengage Learning.

McAdams, T., Neslund, N., Zucker, K. D., & Neslund, K. (2015). *Law, business, and society*. McGraw-Hill Education.

5 Criminal Liability

Figure 5.1 Lady Justice by Arend Ode(Image Credit: AJEL/ pixabay/ Attribution 2.0 Generic (CC BY 2.0))

Chapter Outline

5.1 Common Business Crimes
5.2 Civil vs. Criminal Liability

Introduction

Learning Outcome

- Analyze sources of criminal exposure in business.

5.1 Common Business Crimes

People rarely think about their conduct at work as being potentially illegal, or that jail time could result from poor workplace decisions. However, this fact is the reality. Organizations are fined, and executives are sentenced to jail, when business laws are broken. Many of the workplace violations are nonviolent crimes, such as fraud, property crimes, or drug- or alcohol-related infractions. Regardless of the level of violence or the employee's motivation for committing the crime, breaking the law can lead to negative consequences for the business, its employees, and its customers.

Constitutional Authority to Regulate Business

Congress is given the power to "regulate Commerce with foreign Nations, and among the several States, and with the Indian Tribes." Our forefathers wanted to facilitate easier trade among the states by allowing Congress to adopt rules that could be uniformly applied. The theory was that if commercial enterprises knew that they would be dealing with essentially the same rules across the nation, it would be much easier to run their businesses and keep commerce flowing more efficiently.

While federal courts initially interpreted the commerce power narrowly, over time, the federal courts have decided that the commerce clause gives the federal government broad powers to regulate commerce, not only on an **interstate** (between the states) level, but also on an **intrastate** (within each state) level, as long as some economic transaction is involved. The federal government does not usually exceed its regulatory powers.

White Collar Crime

White collar crimes are characterized by deceit, concealment, or violation of trust. They are committed by business professionals. They generally involve fraud, and the employees committing the crimes are motivated by the desire for financial gains or fear of losing business standing, money, or property. **Fraud** is the intentional misrepresentation of material facts for monetary gain. This type of crime is not dependent on threats or violence.

Figure 5.2 White collar crimes are committed by business professionals within businesses with the intent of gaining or maintaining status. (Credit: Rawpixel/ pexels/ License: CC0)

White collar crimes tend to violate state laws, and sometimes federal laws. The violation depends on what is involved in the crime. For instance, criminal acts involving the United States postal system or interstate commerce violate federal law.

Although white collar crimes do not need to include physical violence, these types of crimes can destroy companies, the environment, and the financial stability of clients, employees, and communities. In 2018, Jeremiah Hand and his brothers, Jehu Hand and Adam Hand, were convicted and sentenced to between 9 and 30 months in prison for their respective roles in a **pump-and-dump** scheme. In this scheme, they were dishonest about control over their company's stock, and even went as far as filing false forms in an effort to raise the value of the stock. Once the value of the stock was raised, they released their shares into the market.

Types of Business Crimes

Business crimes or white collar crimes are not limited to pump-and-dump schemes; they come in many different forms. Business crimes come in many different forms. As previously stated, these crimes often involve deceit, fraud, or misinformation. The types of high-profile crimes include Ponzi schemes, embezzlement, and crimes that intentionally violate environmental laws and regulations. This section will explore these three types of crimes and provide examples from the 2000s.

Ponzi Schemes

Ponzi schemes (also known as pyramid schemes) are investing scams that promise investors low-risk investment opportunities with a high rate of return. The high rates are paid to old investors with money acquired from the acquisition of new investors. The performance of the market is not a factor in the investors' rate of return.

Bernie Madoff operated a 20-year Ponzi scheme through his company. He paid high returns (above average) using the investments of new clients (investors). In 2008, investors attempted to withdraw funds, but the Madoff organization was not able to provide the reimbursement. Madoff is currently serving a more than 100-year sentence in prison.

Larceny and Embezzlement

Larceny and embezzlement are two forms of theft that can occur within a business. **Larceny** occurs when a person unlawfully takes the personal property of another person or a business. For example, if an employee takes another employee's computer with the intent of stealing it, he or she may be guilty of larceny. In contrast, **embezzlement** occurs when a person has been entrusted with an item of value and then refuses to return it or does not return the item. For example, if an employee is entrusted with the petty cash at his or her office and that person purposefully takes some of the money for himself or herself, this would be embezzlement.

One high-profile example of embezzlement occurred at Koss Corporation in Milwaukee, Wisconsin. Sujata "Sue" Sachdeva was a Vice President of Finance and Principal Accounting Officer at Koss Corporation. Sachdeva was convicted of embezzling $34 million over a 5-year period and sentenced to 11 years in federal prison, as well as restitution to Koss Corporation. Sachdeva was entrusted with the company's funds and did not utilize the funds as intended.

Environmental Crimes

Many federal statutes regulate the environment. Many of these laws carry both civil and criminal penalties for violations.

The following federal laws can carry criminal penalties:

- Clean Air Act
- Clean Water Act
- Resource Conservation and Recovery Act
- Comprehensive Environmental Response, Compensation and Liability Act
- Endangered Species Act

The International Petroleum Corporation of Delaware (IPC) is paying restitution for environmental crimes, which included a scheme to violate the Clean Water Act. From 1992 to 2012, IPC processed oil and wastewater.

The company admitted to altering required water test samples so they met the limits set by their permit before releasing the waste into the city's sewer system. The company also admitted to transporting waste that contained benzene, barium, chromium, cadmium, lead, PCE, and trichloroethene for disposal in South Carolina without the required reporting of the information, which also violated environmental laws.

Figure 5.3 White collar crimes are generally motivated by the desire to maintain or gain financial status. (Credit: TheDigitalWay/ pixabay/ License: CC0)

Other Types of Business Crime

The business environment is complex, and some crimes are less common or receive less media attention. These types of crimes include those that violate antitrust laws, racketeering, bribery, money laundering, and spamming.

Violations of Antitrust Laws

Antitrust laws do not allow activities that restrain trade or promote market domination. These laws are in place to provide guidance and supervision of mergers and acquisitions of companies to prevent market abuse. The goal is to avoid **monopolies**, or the control of one organization over a specific market. Monopolies reduce competition and, as a result, can have a detrimental impact on consumer prices. Since the United States is founded on capitalist principles, anti-competitive business conduct is prohibited by law, and some of those laws, such as the Sherman Antitrust Act, do include provisions about criminal punishment.

Racketeering

Racketeering activities include loan-sharking, money laundering, and blackmailing. In the past, the term has been used to describe organized crime. The term is now applied to other entities, as well. RICO, or the Racketeer Influenced and Corrupt Organizations Act, is a federal law aimed at preventing and prosecuting by both businesses and organized crime syndicates. "RICO is now used against insurance companies, stock brokerages, tobacco companies, banks, and other large commercial enterprises." (Schodolski, 2018). Racketeering is no longer limited to organized crime. Health insurance companies and other legitimate businesses are being accused of pressure tactics similar to those used in organized crime racketeering. These claims involve allegations of lying about the actual cost of care, damaging the business for physicians, bullying patients, and attempting to control the doctor-patient relationship through lies and pressure tactics.

Bribery

Bribery occurs when monetary payments, goods, services, information, or anything of value is exchanged for favorable or desired actions. You can be charged with bribery for offering a bribe, or taking a bribe. Bribery is illegal within the United States and outside of it. The Foreign Corrupt Practices Act prohibits bribery payments by U.S. companies to foreign government officials with an intent to influence foreign business results. One example of bribery would be a situation in which a pharmaceutical company offers special benefits to individuals who agree to prescribe their medications.

Money Laundering

Money laundering refers to taking "dirty"money, or money obtained through criminal activities, and passing it through otherwise legitimate businesses so that it appears "clean." The money cannot be tied back to the illegal acts. Clean money is money that was obtained through legitimate business functions.

Spamming

Sending unsolicited commercial email, or **spam**, is illegal. While the onus is on consumers to avail themselves of whatever programs they can to block spam, laws are in place to discourage the sending of spam. The following points are outlined in the anti-spam legislation in Washington state and are similar to other legislation:

1. Individuals may not initiate the sending or plan the sending of an email that misrepresents the sender as someone he or she is not, represents the sender as being associated with an organization that he or she has no association, or otherwise hides the identity of the sender or origin of the email. Email messages may not have false or misleading information in the subject line of the message.
2. Commercial emails must include the contact information of the sender and the receiver must be aware that the message is from a commercial source.

States like Washington are putting legislation in place to reduce spam and asking consumers to take an active role in addressing spam. In general, legislators realize that spam is a nuisance and are finding ways to hold companies liable for sending spam messages.

Conclusion

It is important to know that not all people charged with business crimes or white collar crimes are necessarily guilty. A person must be found guilty of the crime before he or she is convicted. Regardless, business crimes and white collar crimes negatively impact the individual, the organization he or she worked for, the community, and customers.

5.2 Civil vs. Criminal Liability

A legal case can be civil or criminal. Each case has different components and requirements. Before one can understand the civil and criminal systems, it is important to understand the aspects of both civil and criminal laws. The scope, consequences, and treatments of each vary.

Constitutional Rights

It is important to understand the Constitution, which is the basis of all law. States are allowed to create and categorize crimes and punishment, as long as they do not violate rights protected by the U.S. Constitution. For example, in a fairly recent United States Supreme Court case, Lawrence v. Texas, the defendants asserted the unconstitutionality of a Texas law (enacted by the Texas legislature) regarding a particular act. When the United States Supreme Court ruled it unconstitutional, Texas could no longer enforce it.

Frequent issues litigated in the courts are:

- Whether evidence must be suppressed (not allowed to be introduced at trial) because it was obtained pursuant to an unreasonable search and seizure (violating the Fourth Amendment). This category might involve a sub-issue about whether officers had sufficient probable cause to conduct a warrantless search. Without a warrant, and without the suspect's consent, officers generally may only conduct searches if they have "probable cause" to do so; any evidence obtained without consent or probable cause can be objected to, and ultimately ruled inadmissible by the court in trial, if illegally obtained.
- Whether evidence must be suppressed because it was obtained while the suspect was "in custody" without advising a suspect of his rights to remain silent, to speak to an attorney, and to the appointment of an attorney if he cannot afford one (Fifth Amendment privilege against self-incrimination and Sixth Amendment right to counsel), as required by the Supreme Court in the famous Miranda v. Arizona case. The term often used to describe these rights is "Mirandizing," which is named after the case.
- Whether a state law or constitutional provision provides more protection than the U.S. Constitution.

Figure 5.4 Both civil and criminal convictions are based on precedent. (Credit: PactoVisual/ pixabay/ License: CC0)

Components of Crime

There are usually two components to criminal conduct that must be proven by the prosecutor. The prosecutor prosecutes the case against the accused: **mens rea** (the criminal, or guilty, or "wrongful" mind) and **actus reus** (the criminal, or guilty, or "wrongful" act).

Each statute creating a crime is supposed to include a description of:

a. the mental state (**mens rea**) required to establish that the suspect committed the crime, coupled with
b. a description of the conduct (**actus reus**) that the suspect must have done.

The statute generally also indicates the category of crime (felony/misdemeanor/gross misdemeanor).

Criminal Procedures

Generally, the first pleading filed by the prosecutor is called the **information**. (This step could be described as the criminal counterpart to a civil "complaint.")

The next stage is called the **arraignment**, where the defendant appears in court so that the court can determine or confirm his or her identity, inform the defendant of the charge the prosecutor has filed against him or her, and hear the defendant's plea.

Then, there will be discovery and trial. In criminal cases, the jury will convict only if convinced "beyond a reasonable doubt" that the defendant committed the crime, and the verdict must be unanimous. This type of case involves a higher burden of proof than in civil cases.

Criminal and Civil Law

Criminal law addresses behaviors that are offenses against the public, society, or state. Examples of criminal law offenses include assault, drunk driving, and theft. In contrast, **civil laws** address behavior that causes an injury to the private rights of individuals in areas such as child support, divorce, contracts, property, and the person. Examples of civil law offenses include libel, slander, or contract breaches.

Criminal and civil cases differ in who initiates the case, how the case is decided, what punishments or penalties are issued, requirements of proof, and legal protections provided.

Figure 5.5 Civil and criminal cases involve the court system. (Credit: Brett Sayles/ pexels/ License: CC0)

Initiation and Roles

Criminal and civil cases are initiated differently, and the titles of the individuals involved differ slightly. Criminal cases are only initiated by the federal or state government in response to a law being broken. The federal or state governments are known as the prosecution. The prosecution is an attorney, or group of attorneys, hired by the government to present a case against the accused. Criminal cases are usually titled something like "State v. [last name of the defendant accused of a crime]." In criminal prosecutions, the victim is not a party to the lawsuit, but might be a witness for the state at the trial.

In contrast, private parties initiate civil cases when they feel that someone has injured them. Again, civil cases stem from breach of contract, custody cases, and attacks on one's character. Private parties can include an individual, a group, or a business. The person, group, or business who initiates the case is referred to as the plaintiff or complainant. The accused is referred to as the defendant, in both criminal and civil proceedings.

Typically, there is a difference in the burden of proof for the two types of cases. In a criminal case, the defendant must be proven guilty "beyond a reasonable doubt." In a civil case, the defendant must be proven liable through a "preponderance of the evidence." In other words, the prosecution in a civil case must prove that it is more probable than not that the defendant is liable.

In criminal cases, the defendant is entitled to an attorney and may be appointed an attorney if he or she is not able to afford one. The state appoints the attorney. In contrast, all parties involved in a civil case are required to secure their own legal representation.

Typically, civil and criminal laws use different terminology, and being found guilty or accountable in each type of case results in different consequences.

In a civil action (lawsuit), the plaintiff is the person who is alleging that he or she has actually been harmed (physically, financially, or in another manner), and the defendant is the one who is asked to pay damages or otherwise compensate the plaintiff. Outside of financial compensation, the plaintiff may be ordered to do something or refrain from doing something, which is referred to as injunctive relief.

In the Liebeck v. McDonald's case, a woman sued McDonald's for serving hot coffee. The woman spilled hot coffee on her lap while trying to add cream and sugar. The woman sued McDonald's for negligence in a civil suit. The issue centered on whether or not the coffee's specific temperature was unreasonably hot. McDonald's lost the lawsuit. The compensatory verdict was $160,000. McDonald's was found liable.

Conversely, if a defendant is convicted of committing a crime, the consequences are usually incarceration (jail/prison) and/or a fine (payment of money to the state).

The word used to describe the legal responsibility for harm in a civil case is liability, not guilt. Guilty is the word used to describe a person found guilty of committing a crime in a criminal case.

Businesses can be charged with criminal acts as well. In 2017, Oliver Schmidt, former manager of a Volkswagen engineering office near Detroit, was arrested. He faced years in prison for attempts to defraud the United States, wire fraud, violation of the Clean Air Act, and a charge of giving an untrue statement under the Clean Air Act. Schmidt's actions directly violated a business law and, since his actions violated an established law, he was held criminally liable. In December of 2017, Schmidt was sentenced to seven years in prison.

Professional Negligence

Professional negligence is often called **malpractice**. A professional's duty of care is usually a duty to exercise the degree of care, skill, diligence, and knowledge commonly possessed and exercised by a reasonable, careful, and prudent professional of the same type in the state (or sometimes in the community). Along with attorneys and health care providers, the following professionals might be sued for malpractice: accountants, architects, engineers, surveyors, insurance brokers, real estate agents and brokers, and clergy.

For negligence, the usual kind of damages recoverable are **compensatory**, or money to compensate for the injuries/damages incurred to make the person **whole** (e.g., money for medical bills, lost wages, loss of future earning capacity, pain and suffering, emotional distress, property damage, etc.).

Assessment Questions

1. Explain White Collar Crime.

2. What is a pump-and-dump scheme?

3. The crime of larceny includes:

1. The nontresspassory taking and controlling of personal property.
2. The trespassory taking and carrying away of real or personal property.
3. Joyriding.
4. The trespassory taking and control of personal property.

4. Distinguish between larceny and embezzlement.

5. What is the Foreign Corrupt Practices Act?

6. Businesses can be charged with crimes.

a. True.
b. False.

7. The burden of proof is a criminal case is:

a. Reasonable suspicion.
b. Beyond a reasonable doubt.
c. Preponderance of evidence.
d. Clear and convincing evidence.

8. Which of the following is a goal of an arraignment?

a. The defendant is informed of the charge and enters a plea.
b. Requires the defendant to bear the burden of proof
c. Begins the inquisitorial system of adjudication.
d. All of these are correct.

9. The criminal act necessary to commit a crime is known as:

a. Malice aforethought.
b. Mens rea.
c. Subjective fault.
d. Actus reus.

10. Distinguish between civil and criminal law.

Endnotes

Amadeo, Kimberly. Is Social Security a Ponzi Scheme? The Balance Small Business. Retrieved from: https://www.thebalance.com/what-is-a-ponzi-scheme-history-examples-vs-pyramid-scheme-3305877.

CEO of "Penny Stock" Company Sentenced for Stock Manipulation Scheme. The United States Department of Justice. September 11, 2018. Retrieved from: https://www.justice.gov/usao-ma/pr/ceo-penny-stock-company-sentenced-stock-manipulation-scheme.

Schodolski, Vincent J. INSURERS COME UP AGAINST RICO RULE. Chicago Tribune. August 28, 2018. Retrieved from: http://www.chicagotribune.com/news/ct-xpm-2000-06-17-0006170102-story.html.

Verschoor, Curtis C. How an Embezzler Stole Millions from a Small Company. AccountingWEB. January 27, 2011. Retrieved from: https://www.accountingweb.com/aa/law-and-enforcement/how-an-embezzler-stole-millions-from-a-small-company.

White-Collar Crime. FBI. May 03, 2016. Retrieved from: https://www.fbi.gov/investigate/white-collar-crime.

Work Within the Law. Lumen Learning. Retrieved from: https://courses.lumenlearning.com/workwithinthelaw/chapter/categories-and-examples-of-business-crime/.

Duignan, Brian. What Is the Difference Between Criminal Law and Civil Law? Encyclopædia Britannica. Retrieved from: https://www.britannica.com/story/what-is-the-difference-between-criminal-law-and-civil-law.

Civil Law. The Free Dictionary. Retrieved from: https://legal-dictionary.thefreedictionary.com/civil%20law.

Vollman, Brenda, and Borough of Manhattan Community College. Criminal Justice. Lumen Learning. Retrieved from: https://courses.lumenlearning.com/atd-bmcc-criminaljustice/chapter/1-3-the-difference-between-civil-and-criminal-law/.

This OpenStax book is available for free at http://cnx.org/content/col30149/1.5

6 The Tort System

Figure 6.1 (Credit: Free-Photos/ pixabay/ Attribution 2.0 Generic (CC BY 2.0))

Chapter Outline

6.1 Intentional Torts and Negligence

6.2 Product and Strict Liability

Introduction

Learning Outcome

- Explain torts system application to business.

6.1 Intentional Torts and Negligence

Civil suits arise from damages suffered by one or more persons or entities at the hands of another person or entity. The damage can happen in a variety of circumstances, and may be intentional or unintentional. Unlike criminal cases, civil suits seek to provide some form of remedy for the loss suffered by an injured party. Civil suits are decided by judges and juries based on the specific situation, especially when violation of **statutes**, or laws, is not in question.

Figure 6.2 Civil suits are decided in court by judges and juries. (Credit: Coffee/ pixabay/ License: CC0)

Torts

Civil suits involve different causes of action, and they are included in one general classification: **torts**. The word "tort" means "wrong" in French. Thus, torts are wrongs committed against others who suffer some form of damage as a result. While these damages could also be the result of criminal action, the criminal element of the matter is not tried in a civil lawsuit. The standard of proof is lower for civil suits, and a finding of liability in a tort case does not necessarily translate to guilt in a criminal case.

The actor of the wrongs has historically been called a **tortfeasor**. When a wrong is committed by a tortfeasor, damage is done to another. **Tort law** seeks to address this damage based on the circumstances of the issue, which is based on **fault**. Civil lawsuits are used by the injured parties to seek redress for the loss associated with the tort. Unlike criminal proceedings, redress is often provided in the form of money as opposed to incarceration. As such, the burden of proof of fault is lower. The **offender**, or tortfeasor, who commits the act is the accused in a civil suit. The **plaintiff**, who is the injured party, files the lawsuit on which the civil court will make a decision. The offender ultimately becomes the **defendant**, who must respond to the accusations of the plaintiff in a civil suit.

During tort litigation, the judge and jury have certain separate functions (Kionka, 2013):

Functions During a Tort Litigation

The Judge Decides Issues of Law	The Jury Decides Questions of Fact
The duty of the defendant to the plaintiff, if any	What happened

Table 6.1

Functions During a Tort Litigation

The Judge Decides Issues of Law	The Jury Decides Questions of Fact
The elements of the defense	Legal consequences of what happened
Application of legal rules	The damages suffered by the plaintiff

Table 6.1

Harm

Two types of torts are intentional torts and negligence. **Intentional torts** occur as the result of a conscious and purposeful act. **Negligence** occurs when an individual does not exercise duty of care. Torts are acts or omissions that result in injury or **harm** to an individual in such a way that it leads to a civil wrong that occurs as liability (WEX, n.d.). In tort law, harm can be defined as a loss or disadvantage suffered as a result of the actions or omissions of another (WEX, n.d.). This loss can be physical harm, such as slipping and falling on a wet floor, or personal property harm, such as allowing water to ruin furniture. The damage is the result of what someone else did, or did not do, either intentionally or based on a lack of reasonable care.

There are two basic elements to torts: damages and compensation (Laws, tort.laws.com). Tort law acts to compensate persons who have suffered damages at the hands of another (Baime, 2018). Tort law determines the legal responsibility of the defendant and the value of the harm. Different types of torts look at different types of circumstances.

Intentional Torts

Intentional torts are committed by an offender who understands that he or she is committing a tort. Intent does not always equate to directly causing an end result. In some cases, the intent may be something else, such as the possession of knowledge that some harm may occur. The harm may result from intentional action, or due to some circumstance that the offender feels will be excusable (Kionka, 2013).

Some circumstances that could allow the defendant to argue that the action is excusable would include: permission by the injured party, or defense of property, self, or another person (Kionka, 2013). If the injured party agrees to allow the defendant to juggle knives and one slips and causes harm, the action might be excusable to some extent. If a defendant caused harm to the plaintiff's car while trying to avoid being hit by the car, it would likely be excusable.

Different types of intentional torts are based on different circumstances and face different **remedies**, or means of recovering losses (Baime, 2018):

- **Assault** is an intentional tort that occurs when an individual has a reasonable apprehension of an intentional act that is designed to cause harm to himself or herself, or to another person.
- **Malicious prosecution** occurs when an individual files groundless complaints to initiate a criminal matter against another.
- **Defamation** occurs when an individual intentionally creates and promotes malicious falsehoods about another. Defamation can occur in two ways: slander and libel. **Slander** is, in effect, when falsehoods are spoken. **Libel** occurs when falsehoods are expressed in written or other recorded forums.

- **Invasion of privacy** involves unwanted production of negative public information. Different standards apply to invasion of privacy based on the status of the individual as a public figure.

Negligence

Negligence is another type of tort that has two meanings. It is the name of a **cause of action** in a tort, and it is a form of conduct that does not meet the **reasonable standard of care** (Kionka, 2013). The cause of action is the reason for the damage, and the standard of care is based on the care that a reasonable person would need in a given situation. Negligence is decided by determining the duty of the defendant, whether or not the defendant committed a breach of that duty, the cause of the injury, and the injury itself.

For an action to be deemed negligent, there must be a legal **duty of care**, or responsibility to act, based on the reasonable standard in a situation (Baime, 2018). An individual can be considered negligent if he agreed to watch a child, but did not do so, and then harm came to the child. An individual would not be considered negligent if he did not know that he was supposed to watch the child, or did not agree to watch the child.

Figure 6.3 If an individual agrees to watch a child and the child is injured while that person pays attention to her cell phone, it would be considered negligence. (Credit: JESHOOTScom/ pixabay/ License: CC0)

A **reasonable person** is defined as someone who must exercise reasonable care based on what he or she knows about the situation, how much experience he or she has with the situation, and how he or she perceives the situation (Kionka, 2013). In some cases, this knowledge could be based on common knowledge of community matters, such as knowing that a bridge is closed for repairs.

In some cases, the duty of care is based on a **special relationship**, which is a relationship based on an implied duty of care. This implied duty of care often comes about as a **duty to aid**, or a duty to protect another, e.g., a nurse caring for patients in a hospital, or a lifeguard being responsible for swimmers in the guarded area (Baime, 2018). A passerby does not have a duty to aid, but if the individual tries to help, then he or she is responsible for acting responsibly.

The elements of a negligence cause of action are (Kionka, 2013):

- A duty by the defendant to either act or refrain from acting
- A breach of that duty, based on a failure to conform to the standard of care by the defendant
- A causal connection between the defendant's action or inaction, and the injury to the plaintiff
- Measurable harm that can be remedied in monetary damages

Foreseeability

Negligence case decisions are influenced by whether or not a defendant could have predicted that an action or inaction could have resulted in the tort, or **foreseeability** (Baime, 2018). Responsibility is often based on whether or not the harm caused by an action or inaction was **reasonably foreseeable**, which means that the result was fairly obvious before it occurred (Baime, 2018). A person assisting an inebriated individual into her car could be considered negligent due to the likelihood that harm would come to her while she is driving in an intoxicated state. This situation is an example of the **foreseeable probability of harm**.

Conclusion

Intentional torts and negligence arise based on intentional and unintentional acts committed by individuals. Damages are decided in civil courts by first determining fault and harm, and then by assigning a remedy. Sometimes, the damage can be excused if the circumstances indicate that the defendant acted with permission, or in his or her own defense. The main standard used to make a decision is the reasonable standard of care: what would a reasonable person do?

6.2 Product and Strict Liability

Determination of fault and damages for intentional torts and negligence are based on the reasonable standard of care. Another form of torts looks at liability without fault, or **strict liability**. Strict liability determines liability, or harm, based on reasons other than fault (CCBC Legal Studies, n.d.). The mistakes leading to harm can be completely unintentional, and in some cases, unavoidable. Yet, damage is done, and a civil suit arises.

Strict Liability

Strict liability provides a remedy when harm is suffered through no intentional fault. The courts needed to create a standard that would cover this form of tort, or one without fault. The courts came up with the **abnormally dangerous activity standard**, which assigns responsibility when an individual engages in some form of dangerous activity, even if care is taken to avoid mishap (CCBC Legal Studies, n.d.). If a homeowner has horses in a pasture that is bounded by electric fencing, it can be determined that the homeowner exercised reasonable care. However, suppose that the electricity goes down, the horses get out onto the road, and an accident occurs as a result. In this case, the owner is responsible, even though he took reasonable care and the event was unforeseen.

Figure 6.4 If horses get out of a fenced-in area, the owner would be liable for any damage they cause while loose. (Credit: Slack/ pexels/ License: CC0)

For a court to assign strict liability based on abnormally dangerous activities, the activity must meet certain criteria. The court must establish that at least four of the following six factors are present (CCBC Legal Studies, n.d.):

- The activity poses a high degree of risk of harm to a person, the land of another, or the property owned by another.
- The harm resulting from this activity would likely be substantial.
- The use of reasonable care would not eliminate this risk.
- The activity is not something that would be considered a matter of common usage.
- The activity is not appropriate for the place where it occurs.
- The danger of the activity overshadows the benefit it poses to a given community.

In essence, the basis for determining strict liability is the extent of the risk involved in the activity. This basis could also apply to the ownership of dangerous pets. A dog that is known to be aggressive would qualify the owner for strict liability should it get out and bite someone. The courts would find that the owner knew, or should have known, that the dog was dangerous and had a propensity to cause harm (Kionka, 2013).

Trespass

In some situations, the owner of the dangerous activity might not be held liable. One such situation is trespassing. Trespassing occurs as an individual enters or remains upon property owned by another without permission (Kionka, 2013). In the case of trespassing, the owner of the property does not have a duty to make the premises safe based on reasonable care for the trespasser (Kionka, 2013). Also, the owner does not have a responsibility to cancel or alter activities on the premises to avoid endangering the trespasser (Kionka, 2013).

Figure 6.5 Train tracks are a common area for trespassing. (Credit: Muscat_Coach/ pixabay/ License: CC0)

In some cases, however, the property owner could be held liable (Kionka, 2013):

- When the area in question is a common place for trespassing
- When the owner knows a trespasser is present
- When the trespasser needs aid, then the owner has a duty to rescue him or her
- When the trespasser is a child, and the dangerous activity is deemed as an **attractive nuisance**, or an attraction that a reasonable child would wish to view

Even though trespassing can present an exception to liability in the presence of a dangerous activity, it is not a given. There are numerous exceptions that allow for liability. In effect, strict liability can occur in a given situation even when the property owner has provided care that goes above and beyond what is reasonable. The court does not need to establish proof of lack of due care when applying strict liability to a case (Baime, 2018).

Product Liability

Individuals are not always the defendants involved in civil suits. Manufacturers, wholesalers, distributors, and retailers can also be named in torts that pertain to products and qualify as strict liability (CCBC Legal Studies, n.d.). Some products contain flaws that were not intentionally created; such flaws may not be discovered until an individual suffers harm as a result of using them.

It is not always possible to conclusively prove that an act or omission was responsible for the harm (Baime, 2018). As a result, the courts developed the doctrine of **res ipsa loquitor**, which means that whatever it is speaks for itself. The burden of proof shifts from the plaintiff to the defendant, who must disprove negligence. However, the plaintiff must first establish three factors (Baime, 2018):

- The defendant had control over the product in question while it was being manufactured.
- Under normal use and circumstances, the product would not cause damage or harm, but damage or harm has occurred in the case in question.

- The behavior of the plaintiff did not significantly contribute to the harm caused.

The doctrine of res ipsa loquitor does not establish proof of negligence, but it does allow the jury to infer what is not explicitly available pertaining to negligent acts or omissions on the part of the defendant (Baime, 2018).

Negligence can occur when products are created because defects can harm consumers. Think about the potential harm that would occur if brake manufacturers were negligent. This negligence would cause brakes to have flaws, which would prevent them from doing their job of stopping cars. If a car does not stop, people will likely be injured. The manufacturing defect would result in a product liability lawsuit, based on legal responsibility for the harmful consequences proximately caused by the product defect (Baime, 2018). Since the courts would not be able to see the negligence occurring, the courts would base their decision on res ipsa loquitor and the fact that the brakes would not normally fail under normal use by the driver.

Figure 6.6 If brakes do not work like they are supposed to, it could be the result of a manufacturing defect that would result in product liability. (Credit: Valtercirillo/ pixabay/ License: CC0)

The Unreasonably Dangerous Product Standard

In the case of product liability, the court uses an unreasonably dangerous product standard to determine liability. The unreasonably dangerous product would be so dangerous that the danger would be beyond the expectation of the user, and a less dangerous option could have been produced instead (Kionka, 2013). This type of unreasonably dangerous product often falls into one of three categories (Kionka, 2013):

- A flaw in the manufacturing process that occurred because the manufacturer failed to exercise proper care during manufacturing
- A defect in the design of the product, which makes it dangerous, and safer alternatives are available and economically feasible
- The product includes insufficient warnings or instructions for the proper use of the product and its potential dangers

Defenses

There are defenses to product liability claims. In some cases, the plaintiff's own behaviors contribute to his or her injuries, based on his or her own negligence. This situation is known as **contributory negligence**. Contributory negligence, when determined by the court, prevents any recovery of damages by the plaintiff (Baime, 2018). So, if the court finds contributory negligence, the plaintiff is unable to recover any damages for the injury. Two forms of contributory negligence are assumption of risk and misuse.

Assumption of risk is one defense. In some cases, the defendant can argue that the user assumed the risk of using the product if he or she used the product while knowing that the defect in the product created a risk (CCBC Legal Studies, n.d.). An individual who purchases a saw and sees that the guard is too small to cover the teeth, but decides to use it anyway, is assuming the risk of using the product. If the saw cuts the individual, then the manufacturer could argue that the person assumed the risk because he saw the defect, understood the risk, and used the saw anyway.

Another defense is product **misuse**. In some cases, an individual will use a product in ways that it is not meant to be used (CCBC Legal Studies, n.d.). The user might not be aware of a defect, and he or she proceeds to use the product incorrectly. Misuse by the individual would be to blame for any resulting harm.

Figure 6.7 Using a chainsaw with bare feet could be dangerous and add to the risk of use without a guard. If the plaintiff suffered harm because his bare foot could not hold the wood down properly, he could be responsible for comparative negligence. (Credit: edman_eu/ pixabay/ License: CC0)

Plaintiffs might also be responsible for **comparative negligence**. With comparative negligence, the plaintiff's own actions in the use of the product contributed to the harm caused by the product, but the plaintiff might still receive damages (CCBC Legal Studies, n.d.). The amount of negligence on behalf of each part (plaintiff and defendant) is compared to determine the damages to which the plaintiff is entitled (Baime, 2018). If a plaintiff is found to be 30% responsible, and the defendant 70% responsible, then the plaintiff would be entitled to 70% of the damages suffered.

Conclusion

In some cases, a plaintiff suffers harm, but fault is not easily determined, or fault is not the issue. A defendant can exercise reasonable care while the nature of the activity lends itself to risk of harm. Products could have obvious or hidden defects that cause harm to another. When defects occur, the plaintiff has the ability to file a civil suit against the entity that is responsible for the harm-causing defect. The plaintiff might also share some responsibility in the harm, and based on product liability, the court decision will be adjusted accordingly.

Assessment Questions

1. Define Torts.

2. An example of an intentional tort is:

a. Defamation.
b. Assault.
c. Malicious prosecution.
d. All of the above.

3. When an individual creates and promotes malicious falsehoods about another that individual may be liable for:

a. Libel.
b. Slander.
c. Defamation.
d. All of the above.

4. Describe Negligence.

5. All of the following are elements of negligence except:

a. A reasonable person.
b. A duty by the defendant to either act or refrain from acting.
c. A breach of a duty owed by defendant.
d. Measurable harm.

6. Which of the following is a special relationship giving rise to a duty to act to aid or protect one in peril?

a. Hotel and guest.
b. Cousin to cousin.
c. School principal and student.
d. Hotel and guest, and school principal and student.

7. If an activity causes a foreseeable and highly significant risk of physical harm even when reasonable care is exercised by all actors, and the activity is not one of common usage, it is:

a. Proximate cause.
b. Abnormally dangerous.
c. Negligence.
d. None of these are correct.

8. What is an attractive nuisance?

9. The elements of res ipsa loquitor that a plaintiff must establish in a product liability lawsuit include all of the following except:

a. The defendant breached his or her duty of care.
b. The defendant had control over the product in question while it was being manufactured.
c. Under normal circumstances, the product would not cause damage or harm, but damage or harm has occurred in the case in question.
d. The behavior of the plaintiff did not significantly contribute to the harm caused.

10. Describe the differences between contributory and comparative negligence.

Endnotes

Baime. E. (2018). Fundamentals of tort law. Retrieved from: https://nationalparalegal.edu/FundamentalsTortLaw.aspx.

Cornell Law School. (n.d.). Tort. Retrieved from: https://www.law.cornell.edu/wex/tort.

Kionka, E. J. (2013). Torts (5th ed.). St. Paul, MN: West Academic Publishing. Retrieved from: https://lscontent.westlaw.com/images/content/Torts5th.pdf.

Baime. E. (2018). Fundamentals of tort law. Retrieved from: https://nationalparalegal.edu/FundamentalsTortLaw.aspx.

CCBC Legal Studies (n.d.) Strict liability. Retrieved from: https://ccbclegalstudiesbusinesslaw.wordpress.com/unit-1-foundations-of-law/torts/strict-liability/.

Kionka, E. J. (2013). Torts (5th ed.). St. Paul, MN: West Academic Publishing. Retrieved from: https://lscontent.westlaw.com/images/content/Torts5th.pdf.

7 Contract Law

Figure 7.1 (Credit: edar/ pixabay/ Attribution 2.0 Generic (CC BY 2.0))

Chapter Outline

7.1 Consideration and Promissory Estoppel
7.2 Capacity and Legality
7.3 Breach of Contract and Remedies

Introduction

Learning Outcome

- Analyze the principles of contract law and how they apply to businesses.

7.1 Consideration and Promissory Estoppel

A contract is defined as an agreement between two or more parties that is enforceable by law.

To be considered enforceable by law, a contract must contain several elements, including offer and acceptance, genuine agreement, consideration, capacity, and legality.

Figure 7.2 Before a contract can become legal and enforceable, several elements must first be in place. (Credit: rawpixel/ pixabay/ License: CC0)

The key to a contract is that there must be an offer, and acceptance of the terms of that offer. An offer is a proposal made to demonstrate an intent to enter a contract. Acceptance is the agreement to be bound by the terms of the offer. Offers must be made with intent, must be definite and certain (i.e., the offer must be clearly expressed for it to be enforceable), and must be communicated to the offeree. An acceptance must demonstrate the willingness to consent to all of the terms of the offer.

Genuine agreement, i.e., "a meeting of the minds," is also required. Agreement can be destroyed by fraud, misrepresentation, mistake, duress, or undue influence.

Consideration must be included in contracts. Consideration is a thing of value promised in exchange for something else of value. This mutual exchange binds the parties together.

Capacity to contract is the next element required for a valid agreement. The law presumes that anyone entering a contract has the legal capacity to do so. Minors are generally excused from contractual responsibility, as are mentally incompetent and drugged or drunk individuals.

Finally, legality is the last element considered. Parties entering into contracts that involve illegal conduct may not expect judicial relief to have that contract enforced. This theory has also been applied to conduct that would be considered in opposition to public policy.

Consideration and Promissory Estoppel

Contract law employs the principles of consideration and promissory estoppel.

Consideration

In most cases, consideration need not be pecuniary (monetary). Most contracts are enforceable only if each party gets consideration from the agreement. Consideration can be money, property, a promise, or some right. For instance, when a music company sells studio equipment, the promised equipment is the consideration for the buyer. The seller's consideration is the money the buyer promises to pay for the equipment.

Promissory Estoppel

The promissory estoppel doctrine is an exception to the requirement of consideration for contracts. Promissory estoppel is triggered when one party acts on the other party's promise. In cases where it is triggered, there is harm or severe injustice to the party who acted because they relied on the other party's broken promise.

The doctrine of promissory estoppel allows aggrieved parties to pursue justice or fairness for the performance of a contract in court, or other equitable remedies, even in the absence of any consideration. Its legal application may vary from state to state, but the basic elements include:

- A legal relationship existed between the parties.
- A promise was made.
- There was reliance on the promise that caused one party to act before any real consideration was exchanged.
- A substantial and measurable detriment occurred as a result of the failure to perform on the contract.
- An unconscionable result, or gross injustice, resulted from the broken promise.

If it is found that these elements are satisfied and that the doctrine of estoppel is applicable, then the court will issue the appropriate damages in the form of reliance damages to restore the aggrieved party to the position they were in prior to the broken promise. Expectation damages are not usually available if promissory estoppel is being claimed.

An example of how this principle would apply is:

EXAMPLE 7.1

After a bidding war for his services, Bob turns down a job offer with We are the Best, LLC in Miami, Florida (where he lives), and accepts a dream job offer from MegaCorp Co. in San Francisco, California. The offer contains a specific start date, compensation terms, benefits outline, and more. However, it does not include relocation expenses or provisions. The company is aware of his plans to move across the country for the sole purpose of taking this dream role. Bob breaks his Miami lease with penalty and spends approximately $13,000 in moving and travel costs. As the cost of living in San Francisco is much higher than in Miami, he puts down a much pricier first and last month's rent and security deposit payment than he is used to. Within two days of his planned start date, he receives a call from management at MegaCorp Co. stating that the company has changed its mind and decided to go in a different direction. If Bob brings a promissory estoppel suit, he will likely be entitled to all of the costs that he incurred while anticipating the start of the promised role (i.e., penalty for the broken lease, moving costs, difference in the rental costs, cost of breaking the new lease, if necessary, etc.) Following reimbursement of his costs, Bob will be returned to the same position he was in prior to the broken promise. However, the company will not likely be required to reopen the role for him or give him the job, as originally anticipated. Also, he will not likely be awarded any damages for the job that he turned down with We are the Best, LLC, as expectation damages are not usually available.

The doctrines of consideration and promissory estoppel are essential to an understanding of how contracts are formed and enforced in the United States.

7.2 Capacity and Legality

For a contract to be legally binding, the parties entering into the contract must have the **capacity** to do so. As a legal matter, there are certain classes of people who are presumed to have no capacity to contract. These include legal minors, the mentally ill, and those who are intoxicated. If people meeting these criteria enter into a contract, the agreement is considered **voidable**. If a contract is voidable, then the person who lacked capacity has the choice to either end the contract or continue with it as agreed upon. This design is meant to protect the party lacking capacity.

Following are some examples of the application of these rules.

Minors Have No Capacity to Contract

In most states, minors under the age of 18 lack the capacity to make a contract and may therefore either honor an agreement or void the contract. However, there are a few exceptions to this rule. In most states, a contract for necessities (i.e. food and clothing) may not be voided. Also, in most states, the contract can no longer be voided when the minor turns 18.

EXAMPLE 7.2

Mary, 16, an athlete, signs a long-term endorsement deal with a well-known brand and is compensated for several years. At age 20, she decides she wants to take a better endorsement deal, so she tries to void the agreement on the grounds that it was made when she was a minor and that she lacked capacity at that time. Mary will not likely succeed in having her agreement voided, as she has passed the period of incapacity.

Mental Incapacity

If a person lacks the mental capacity to enter a contract, then either he or she, or his or her legal guardian, may void it, except in cases where the contract involved necessities. In most states, mental capacity is measured against the "cognitive standard" of whether the party understood its meaning and effect.

EXAMPLE 7.3

Mr. Williams contracted to sell a patent. Later, however, he claimed that he lacked capacity to enter the agreement. He, therefore, sought to have the contract voided. Williams based his claim on the fact that he had been diagnosed as manic-depressive and had received treatment from a variety of mental hospitals for this condition. His doctor stated that he was unable to properly evaluate business opportunities and contracts while in a "manic" state. A California Court of Appeals, evaluating a similar situation, refused to terminate the contract and stated that even in his manic state, the party was capable of contracting, as his condition may have impaired his judgment but not his understanding of the contract. With other mental conditions, a different legal conclusion could be reached.

Voluntary Intoxication – Drugs and Alcohol

Courts generally do not find lack of capacity to contract for people who are voluntarily intoxicated. The rationale for this decision is found in the reasoning that individuals should not be allowed to side-step their contractual obligations by virtue of their self-induced states. By another token, however, courts also seek to avoid the undesirable result of allowing the sober party to take advantage of the other person's condition. Therefore, if a party is so inebriated that he or she is unable to understand the nature and consequences of the agreement, then the contract may be voided by the inebriated party.

EXAMPLE 7.4

In the late 1900s, the owner of a significant amount of stock went on a three-month drinking binge. A local bank that was aware of his consistent inebriation hired a third party to contract with him. The third party succeeded in getting him to sell his stock for about 1.5% of the worth of its total value. When the duped seller ended his binge a month later, he learned that the third party had sold the stock to the local bank behind the deal. He then sued the third party. Ultimately, the case was decided by the U.S. Supreme Court, which found that the agreement was void because both the bank and the third party knew that the plaintiff was unaware of what he was doing when he entered the contract. The bank was required to return the shares to the plaintiff, minus the 1.5% amount of real value that he had been paid for the shares.

Legality

Contracts must be created for the exchange of legal goods and services to be enforced. An agreement is void if it violates the law, or is formed for the purpose of violating the law. Contracts may also be found voidable if they are found violative of public policy, although this is rarer. Typically, this conclusion is only invoked in clear cases where the potential harm to the public is substantially incontestable, eluding the idiosyncrasies of particular judges.

For a contract to be binding, it must not have a criminal or immoral purpose or go against public policy. For example, a contract to commit murder in exchange for money will not be enforced by the courts. If performing the terms of the agreement, or if formation of the contract, will cause the parties to engage in activity that is illegal, then the contract will be deemed illegal and will be considered void or "unenforceable," similar to a nonexistent contract. In this case, there will not be any relief available to either party if they breach the contract. Indeed, it is a defense to a breach of contract claim that the contract itself was illegal.

EXAMPLE 7.5

In a state where gambling is illegal, two parties enter into an employment contract for the hiring of a blackjack dealer. The contract would be void because the contract requires the employee to perform illegal gambling activities. If the blackjack dealer tries to recover any unpaid wages for work completed, his claim will not be recognized because the courts will treat the contract as if it never existed.

By contrast, parties enter a contract that involves the sale of dice to a known dealer in a state where gambling is unlawful. The contract would not be considered void because the act of selling dice, in and of itself, is not illegal.

Some examples of contracts that would be considered illegal are contracts for the sale or distribution of illegal drugs, contracts for illegal activities such as loansharking, and employment contracts for the hiring of undocumented workers.

An understanding of the several theories outlined herein for establishing (or challenging) capacity and legality in contract law is essential to this area of law.

7.3 Breach of Contract and Remedies

Once a contract is legally formed, both parties are generally expected to perform according to the terms of the contract. A breach of contract claim arises when either (or both) parties claim that there was a failure, without legal excuse, to perform on any, or all, parts and promises of the contract.

Several inquiries are triggered when a breach of contract claims is initiated. The first step is to determine whether a contract existed in the first place. If it did, the following questions may be asked: What did the terms of the contract require of the parties? Were the contractual terms modified at any point? Did the breach actually occur? Was the claimed breach material to the contract? Does any legal excuse or defense to enforcement of the contract exist? What damages were caused by the breach?

Material vs. Minor Breach

The parties' obligations and remedies for a breach of contract depend on whether the breach is considered material or minor.

When something substantially different from what was expected under the terms of the contract is delivered, the breach will be considered material. For example, the breach will be considered material if the contract promises the delivery of Christmas ornaments, but the buyer receives a box of candies. In the case of a material breach, the non-breaching party has the right to all remedies for breach of the entire contract and is no longer expected to perform their obligations. In considering whether a breach is material, courts will determine whether the non-breaching party still received a benefit, and if so, how much was received, adequate compensation for the damages, the extent of the performance (if any) by the breaching party, any hardship to the breaching party, the negligence or intent behind the behavior of the breaching party, and finally, the possibility that the breaching party will perform the remainder of the contract.

There are times, however, that despite the breaching party's failure to perform some of the contract, the other party still receives a majority of the goods or services specified in the contract. In this case, the breach will be considered minor. For example, the breaching party may be late on delivering goods or services promised under a contract that does not specify a firm delivery date and that doesn't state that time is of the essence. In this case, a reasonably short delay would likely only be considered a minor breach of the contract. Consequently, the non-breaching party would still be required to perform as pursuant to the contract. However, damages may be available to them if they suffered some harm as a result of the delay.

Remedies

Typically, the remedies that will be available if a breach of contract is found are money damages, restitution, rescission, reformation, and specific performance.

Figure 7.3 When there is a breach of contract, the courts might get involved to help determine the remedy. (Credit: succo/ pixabay/ License: CC0)

Money damages include compensation for financial losses caused by the breach.

Restitution restores the injured party to status quo or the position they had prior to the formation of the contract, by returning to the plaintiff any money or property given pursuant to the contract. This type of relief is typically sought when a contract is voided by courts due to a finding that the defendant is incompetent or lacks capacity.

Rescission or reformation may be available to parties who enter into contracts by mistake, fraud, undue influence, or duress. Rescission terminates the duties of both parties under the contract, while reformation allows courts to equitably change the contract's substance.

Specific performance compels one party to perform the promises stated in the contract as nearly as practicable. Specific performance is only mandated when money damages do not adequately compensate for the breach. Personal service, however, may not be used to compel specific performance, since doing so would constitute forced labor, i.e. slavery, which is in violation of the U.S. Constitution.

Inevitably, when valid contracts are created, the potential for breach exists. An understanding of what happens when a contract's terms are breached is fundamental to an understanding of contract law.

Assessment Questions

1. What is the definition of a contract?

2. The elements of a contract include all but the following element:

a. Offer and acceptance.
b. Consideration.
c. Capacity.
d. Promissory Estoppel.

3. What are the ways an agreement can be invalidated?

a. Fraud.
b. Misrepresentation.
c. Undue influence.
d. All of the above.

4. Describe the concept of Promissory Estoppel.

5. Consideration may include any of the following except:

a. A promise.
b. A gift.
c. Property.
d. Money.

6. What happens when a person lacks the legal capacity to enter into a contract?

7. Which of the following is most likely to be classified as a necessity for which a minor will be held liable on a contract?

a. A television.
b. School supplies.
c. Education.
d. Food.

8. A minor can avoid a contract to purchase a car if:

a. The car has been destroyed.
b. The car has been damaged.
c. He or she grows tired of it.
d. All of the above.

9. When can a mentally incompetent person void a contract?

10. Examples of illegal contracts include all but the following:

a. Contracts for the sale or distribution of heroin.
b. Contracts for loansharking.
c. Contracts in consideration of marriage.
d. Employment contracts for the hiring of undocumented workers.

11. Define a material breach.

12. Typical remedies available for a breach of contract include:

a. Money damages.
b. Rescission.
c. Specific Performance.
d. All of the above.

13. Distinguish between rescission and reformation.

14. Courts of equity will not grant specific performance of contracts:

a. For a personal service contract.
b. For the sale of real estate.
c. For the sale of the original manuscript of a rare edition book.
d. All of these are correct.

15. Define restitution.

Endnotes

Promissory Estoppel: Requirements and Limitations of the Doctrine. University of Pennsylvania Law School. Retrieved from: https://scholarship.law.upenn.edu/cgi/viewcontent.cgi?article=9407&context=penn_law_review.

Promissory Estoppel as a Substitute for Consideration. *LawShelf Educational Media*. Retrieved from: https://lawshelf.com/videos/entry/contract-law-promissory-estoppel-as-a-substitute-for-consideration.

US Legal, Inc. Consideration. Contracts. Retrieved from: https://contracts.uslegal.com/consideration/.

Stim, R. Consideration: Every Contract Needs It. Nolo. 23 Apr. 2015. Retrieved from: www.nolo.com/legal-encyclopedia/consideration-every-contract-needs-33361.html.

What Is 'Consideration' and How Much Is Required? *Findlaw*. Retrieved from: https://smallbusiness.findlaw.com/business-contracts-forms/what-is-consideration-and-how-much-is-required.html.

Bradley, J. The Legal Capacity of a Contract. November 21, 2017. Retrieved from: https://smallbusiness.chron.com/legal-capacity-contract-62816.html.

Capacity To Enter Into Contracts – Contract Law. https://laws.com/. Retrieved from: https://contract-law.laws.com/legality/capacity-to-enter-into-contracts.

Can a Minor Enter into a Contract? HG.org. Retrieved from: https://www.hg.org/legal-articles/can-a-minor-enter-into-a-contract-34024.

Breach of Contract, Remedies that can be Pursued. HG.org. Retrieved from: https://www.hg.org/legal-articles/breach-of-contract-legal-remedies-that-can-be-pursued-22797.

Remedies for Breaches of Contract. LawTeacher. Retrieved from: https://www.lawteacher.net/free-law-essays/contract-law/remedies-for-breaches-of-contract-law-essay.php.

Contracts—termination and contractual claims and remedies—overview. Lexis PSL. Retrieved from: https://www.lexisnexis.com/uk/lexispsl/bankingandfinance/document/391289/5FKM-GJ81-F185-X1CM-00000-00/Contracts_termination_and_contractual_claims_and_remedies_overview.

8 Sales Contracts

Figure 8.1 (Credit: JESHOOTS-com/ pixabay/ Attribution 2.0 Generic (CC BY 2.0))

Chapter Outline

8.1 The Nature and Origins of Sales Contracts
8.2 Warranties and Sales Contracts

Introduction

Learning Outcome

- Recognize nuances of contracts pertaining to sales.

8.1 The Nature and Origins of Sales Contracts

Features of Sales Contracts

Commercial enterprises that engage in buying and selling practices need to be aware of the features and nature of **sales contracts**. A contract of sale is a specific type of contract in which one party is obligated to deliver and transfer ownership of a good to a second party, who in turn is obligated to pay for the good in money, or its equivalent. The party who is obligated to deliver the good is known as the **vendor** or seller. The party who is obligated to pay for the good is known as the **vendee** or buyer.

It has generally been established that there are six main features of sales contracts. Sales contracts are:

1. **Consensual**: they are perfected by mere consent without the need for any additional acts
2. **Bilateral**: both parties in the contract are bound to fulfill reciprocal obligations toward each other
3. **Onerous**: the good sold is conveyed in consideration of the price, and the price paid is conveyed in consideration of the good

4. **Commutative**: the good sold is considered to be the equivalent of the price, and vice versa
5. **Nominate**: this type of contract has a special designation (i.e., sale)
6. **Principal**: the validity does not depend upon the existence of other contracts

Sources of Law for Sales Contracts

Only in very limited circumstances (such as in the buying and selling of stocks) does federal law govern sales contracts. Until the 1950s, there were two main sources of law for sales contracts: state common law and state statutory law. Thus, the laws governing sales contracts differed from state to state. As interstate commercial activity grew in importance, there was a need for a uniform law for sales transactions that would harmonize rules across the states. Therefore, in 1952, the **Uniform Commercial Code** (**UCC**)was created to govern business transactions. All 50 states have adopted the Code, but each has the power to modify it, in line with the wishes of the state legislature.

The Uniform Commercial Code

The UCC categorizes items that can be bought or sold into three types:

1. **Goods** are defined in Section 2-105 of the UCC as tangible items "which are movable at the time of identification to the contract for sale." Therefore, the primary features of goods are that they are movable and tangible. Refrigerators, paper, and furniture are all examples of goods.
2. **Services** are items that are movable but not tangible. Accounting is an example of a service.
3. **Realty** describes non-good items that are tangible but not movable. Under this definition, commercial and residential property are classed as realty.

These definitions have created some grey areas that have been clarified by the courts in their interpretation of the UCC. In the 2008 case Crown Castle Inc. et al. v. Fred Nudd Corporation et al., a case in which the telecommunications company Crown Castle sued a cell phone tower installation firm for the construction of faulty towers, the courts had to determine whether cell phone towers (monopoles) should be classified as movable (and hence goods) or non-movable (and therefore realty). Ultimately, it was determined that monopoles are goods. Items that are attached to realty (e.g. a counter or a bar) and that are used for business activities are described as **trade fixtures** and treated as goods. Software licenses are not tangible, but they are also not movable, and have been treated in different ways: as goods, a **mixed sale** (a tangible item tied to an intangible item), and pure services. Items such as soil and clay may be treated as goods even if they are part of immovable land because they can be extracted and moved. Crops that are sold while they are still growing on the land are also considered to be goods even though they are technically immovable while growing.

Article 2 of the UCC specifically pertains to sales contracts of goods. It defines a sale as a transaction that involves "the passing of title from the seller to the buyer for a price." However, **merchants** are classified as a separate entity under the terms of the UCC. This distinction is important because the Code contains provisions that specifically apply to merchants and place greater duties on merchants to protect private citizens. There are four ways in which an entity can be classified as a merchant:

Classification	Examples

Table 8.1

This OpenStax book is available for free at http://cnx.org/content/col30149/1.5

An agent who regularly sells goods as part of his or her business or trade	A seller on an online auction site
An individual who employs other people to sell goods	The owner of a clothing store
A person who works for a person who sells goods	An employee at a grocery retailer
Any entity who self-identifies as a merchant	An individual who describes himself or herself as a merchant in corporate documents

Table 8.1

Formation of Sales Contracts under the UCC

Sales contracts require most of the same components as general contracts, but the UCC includes some provisions that specifically pertain to the creation of sales contracts. First, the UCC includes a new category of **offer**. Basic contract law states that for an offer to be valid, it has to have "definiteness of terms." In the UCC, most of that particular rule is modified for greater flexibility. If the parties have "open" (in other words, "not definite") terms, the UCC addresses the situation with an overlay of "reasonableness"—for example, if no time for performance is designated, the performance must occur within a "reasonable" time. As a result, the following terms are legally allowed to be "open," and there is a "default" provision that will apply under the UCC:

Open Term	Default	Applicable UCC Provision
Price	If price is not named, the default is "reasonable price."	UCC 2-305(1)
Payment	If payment is not named, default is "due at the time and place at which the buyer is to receive the goods."	UCC 2-310(a)
Delivery	If delivery is not named, the default is "buyer normally takes delivery at the seller's place of business."	UCC 2-308(a)
Duration of an Ongoing Contract	If duration of an ongoing contract is not named, the default is "buyer normally takes delivery at the seller's place of business."	UCC 2-308(a)

Table 8.2

The only term that really *cannot* be left open is the **quantity** term. The court is not going to second-guess a quantity if the parties don't set one in the contract—for example, why would the court arbitrarily want to force the parties to buy and sell 15,000 widgets if a quantity wasn't specified? There are two exceptions to this rule: **requirements contracts** ("as much as I need") and **output contracts** ("as much as you can produce"). Even though these ideas are **illusory**, they're generally allowed in the commercial setting with good-faith limitations under UCC 2-306.

Sometimes, however, the courts will not allow purported "requirements" contracts. In one case, a court ruled that the contract was an unenforceable illusory contract instead of an enforceable requirements contract, even though it was a contract for the sale of goods ("as much as I need"). The reason for this ruling was that it did not appear that the buyer had any real intention of going through with any purchase.

Under Section 2-205 of the UCC, offers made by merchants are considered to be **firm offers** if the offers are made in writing and explicitly state that there is a three-month irrevocability period. A three-month irrevocability period is assumed if no mention is made with the offer. **Acceptance** of the offer can be made in any reasonable manner, but the **mirror-image rule** does not apply under the UCC. This means that if the terms of the acceptance do not mirror those of the offer, the acceptance is treated as a counteroffer and no legal contract is formed. Sale of goods contracts must be in writing if the value of the goods is $500 or more. Modifications to the contract must be made in good faith, and new consideration is not required. A contract provision, or the entire contract itself, can be considered to be **unconscionable** if its terms are unfair or unreasonable. If a court deems this to be the case, the contract, or certain provisions of it, may be unenforceable.

Title

Title means ownership of a good. When the sale is completed, an agent must pass the title for the good to the buyer. There are three types of titles:

1. **Good title** describes a title that is obtained from an individual who owns the goods free and clear.
2. **Void title** occurs when the title is passed to the buyer from a person who does not legitimately own the title. An important point is that good faith is irrelevant when a void title is acquired. For example, a person who unknowingly purchased stolen goods has a void title. An exception occurs when an owner **entrusts** goods to a merchant who ordinarily deals in those goods, and then that merchant sells the goods to a good-faith buyer. In this case, the buyer acquires a good title. For example, if a motorcycle owner takes the motorcycle to a vehicle repair shop and the motorcycle is accidentally sold, the buyer acquires the title.
3. **Voidable title** occurs when the contract would have been good, but certain circumstances make it voidable. For example, if the buyer was deceitful about his or her true identity, the buyer is a minor, or the buyer wrote a bad check in the sale, then the title is deemed voidable.

This OpenStax book is available for free at http://cnx.org/content/col30149/1.5

Figure 8.2 A sale is defined as a transaction that involves the passing of a title from the seller to the buyer for a price. (Credit: Negative Space/ pexels/ License: CC0)

Issues Associated with Title

Imagine the following scenario: A café purchases a new coffee machine from a supplier. However, when the supplier tries to deliver the equipment to the café, it is involved in an accident and the coffee machine is destroyed. A question emerging from this scenario is this: Is the supplier legally obligated to replace the machine? Asked differently: Who holds the good title in this scenario?

Prior to the introduction of the Uniform Common Code, the loss would have fallen on the owner of the café, since he or she paid for the coffee machine prior to taking possession of it. Under the UCC, however, as long as the supplier is considered a merchant, the risk of loss remains with the merchant until the buyer takes possession of the good.

Given problems like the one described above, the UCC separately considers four specific issues relating to titles:

- **Ownership**. Under consideration is the question of *when* the title transfers from vendor to vendee, and hence when ownership is said to occur.
- The concept of **encumbrance** considers when the vendee is granted an interest in the good such that the good can be used as collateral for a debt.
- The UCC considers when the risk of **loss** attaches and what the responsibilities of the buyer and seller are to each other, should a loss occur.
- **Insurable interest** is the right to insure the goods against exposure to risk of loss or damage

The UCC allows four scenarios for sales contracts: simple delivery contracts, common-carrier delivery contracts, goods-in-bailment contracts, and conditional sales contracts.

Each type involves the title, risk of loss, and insurable interest passing at different times.

A **simple delivery contract** occurs when the goods are transferred from the buyer to the seller at the time of the sale or later, e.g., if the goods are delivered. Title transfers when the contract is executed, insurable interest passes at the same time, and risk of loss transfers when the buyer takes possession, unless the seller is not a merchant. In the latter case, under the rule of **tender of delivery**, risk remains with the buyer.

A **common-carrier delivery contract** occurs when a common carrier, who is an independent contractor rather than an agent of the seller (e.g., a trucking line), delivers the goods. The UCC further categorizes these types of contracts into shipment contracts and destination contracts:

1. A **shipment contract** occurs when it is the responsibility of the seller to make the shipping arrangements and to transfer the goods to the common carrier. Under this contract, title passes to the buyer at the time of shipment, so the buyer bears the risk of loss, even when he or she has not taken possession of the goods.
2. A **destination contract** occurs when the seller is required to deliver the goods to a location that is stipulated in the contract. Under this contract, title transfers when the goods are delivered, but the seller bears the risk of loss until that time.

A **goods-in-bailment contract** occurs when the goods are stored under the control of a third party, such as in a warehouse or on a ship. Transfer of title and risk of loss depends on whether the seller has a document indicating ownership of the goods and whether that document is negotiable or non-negotiable. A **negotiable** document contains the words, "deliver to the order of [seller]." As soon as that document is endorsed to the buyer, both title and risk pass to the buyer. A **non-negotiable** document lacks those words. Under these circumstances, title passes with the endorsement of the document, but risk of loss does not pass until the custodian of the goods is notified of the title. If a document of title is completely absent, title passes at the same time as the execution of the contract, but risk does not pass until the custodian is notified of, and acknowledges, the transaction. Insurable interest is created when either the buyer or seller has the title, risk of loss, or an economic interest in the goods.

Finally, a **conditional sales contract** is a contract that occurs when the sale is dependent on approval. For example, a sale-or-return agreement occurs when both parties agree that the buyer can return the goods at a later date. Insurable interest is created once the goods are identified in the contract. Title and risk of loss depend on whether the goods are delivered by the common carrier, the seller, or in bailment, as described above.

The International Sale of Goods

With globalization, there has been a significant expansion of commercial transactions undertaken across international borders. The **United Nations Convention on Contracts for the International Sale of Goods**, or the CISG, is the main legal structure offered for the governance of international commercial transactions. The CISG broadly covers the same topics as the UCC, but it preempts the UCC if there is a problem with an international sale.

8.2 Warranties and Sales Contracts

Figure 8.3 The law provides remedies for breach of sales contracts. (Credit: rawpixel/ pexels/ License: CC0)

Warranties

A **warranty** is a guarantee on the good that comes as part of the sales contract, but contract law treats warranties as an additional form of contract that binds the selling party to undertake a certain action. Typically, the selling party has an obligation to provide a product that achieves a specified task, or to deliver a service that meets certain minimal standards. Warranties are offered for a range of different goods and services, from manufactured goods to real estate to plumbing services. The warranty assures the buyer that the good or service is free from defects, and it is a legally binding commitment. In the event that the product or service fails to meet the standards set out in the warranty, then the contract provides a specific remedy, such as a replacement or repair.

According to UCC 1-203, the performance and execution of all contracts must be undertaken in good faith. **Good faith** means honesty in fact and the observance of reasonable commercial standards of fair dealing. If the parties in the contract are merchants, the UCC also requires that the contract be undertaken in accordance with **commercial reasonableness.** This requirement means that the transaction should be undertaken in a sensible and prudent way.

Express and Implied Warranties

Warranties can be express, implied, or both. Both express and implied warranties provide legal relief for the purchaser in the event of a breach of contract.

An **express warranty** is one in which the seller explicitly guarantees the quality of the good or service sold. Typically, the vendor provides a statement, or other binding document, as part of the sales contract. What this means in practice is that the buyer has engaged in the contract on the reasonable assumption that the quality, nature, character, purpose, performance, state, use, or capacity of the goods or services are the same as those stated by the seller. Therefore, the sales contract is based, in part, on the understanding that the goods or services being supplied by the seller will conform to the description, or any sample, that has been provided.

There are myriad ways in which the seller can make statements as to the characteristics of the goods.

Here are a few examples of express warranties:

"Wrinkle-free shirt"

"Lifetime guarantee"

"Made in the USA"

"This orange juice is not from concentrate"

"24k gold"

There is not a specific way that words must be formed to make an express warranty valid. Importantly, the sales contract does not need to explicitly state that a warranty is being intended. It is enough that the seller asserts facts about the goods that then become part of the contract between the parties. However, the courts do apply a **reasonableness test of reliance** upon warranties. Puffery, or language used to bolster sales, is lawful, and the consumer is required to apply reason when evaluating such statements. For example, buyers are expected to use reason when judging seller claims such as "this sandwich is the best in the world." Obvious sales talk cannot ordinarily be treated as a legally binding warranty.

A **breach** of the warranty occurs when the express warranty has been found to be false. In such circumstances, the warrantor is legally liable just as though the truth of the warranty had been guaranteed. The courts do not accept as a defense:

- Seller claims the warranty was true.
- Seller claims due care was exercised in the production or handling of the product.
- Seller claims there is not any reason to believe that the warranty was false.

Implied Warranties

In certain circumstances where no express warranty was made, the law **implies** a warranty. This statement means that the warranty automatically arises from the fact that a sale was made. With regard to implied warranties, the law distinguishes between casual sellers and merchant sellers, with the latter held to a higher standard, given that they are in the business of buying or selling the good or service rendered. For example, unless otherwise agreed, goods sold by merchants carry an implied warranty against claims by any third party by way of trademark infringement, patent infringement, or any other intellectual property law infringement. This type of warranty is known as the **warranty against infringement.** Another implied warranty provided by merchant sellers is the **warranty of fitness for normal use**, which means that the goods must be fit for the ordinary purposes for which they are sold.

It is important to note that if express warranties are made, this does not preclude implied warranties. If an express warranty is made, it should be consistent with implied warranties, and can be treated as cumulative, if such a construction is reasonable. If the express and implied warranties cannot be construed as **consistent** and **cumulative**, the express warranty generally prevails over the implied warranty, except in the case of the implied **warranty of merchantability**, or fitness for purpose.

Breaches of Warranty

If the buyer believes that there has been a breach of the implied warranty of merchantability, it is their responsibility to demonstrate that the good was defective, that this defect made the good not fit for purpose, and that this defect caused the plaintiff harm. Typical examples of defects are:

- Design defects
- Manufacturing defects
- Inadequate instructions on the use of the good
- Inadequate warning against the dangers involved in using the good.

Specific Examples of Goods Under the Warranty of Merchantability

Type	Description
Second-hand goods	The UCC treats warranties arising for used goods in the same way as warranties arising for new goods, but second-hand products tend to be held to a lower standard on the warranty of merchantability.
Buyer-designed goods	The same warranties arise for mass manufactured goods as for goods that have been specified or made to order for the buyer. However, in this case, no warranty of fitness for purpose can arise since the buyer is using his or her own decisions, skill, and judgment when making the purchase.
Food and drink	The sale of food or drink carries the implied warranty of being fit for human consumption.

Table 8.3

The buyer might intend to use the goods purchased for a different purpose than that for which it was sold. In this case, the implied warranty holds only if the buyer relies on the seller's skill or judgment to select the product, the buyer informs the seller at the time of purchase of his or her intention for the use of the good, and the buyer relies on the seller's judgment and skill in making the final choice. If the seller is not made aware of the buyer's true intention, or does not offer his or her skill and judgment in aiding the sale, then warranty of fitness for a particular purpose does not arise. For this reason, it is common for vendors to include provisions in the average terms and conditions of sale with regard to the true and intended purpose of use.

Warranty of Title

By the mere act of selling, the vendor implies a warranty that the title is good and that the transfer of title is lawful. In addition, the act of the sale creates a warranty that the goods shall be delivered free from any lien of which the buyer was unaware. In some circumstances, the warranty of title can be excluded from the contract documents. For instance, when the seller makes the sale in a representative capacity (e.g. as an executor of an estate), then a warranty of title will not arise.

Remedies to Buyers under the UCC

Remedy	Description
Cancel the contract	The UCC allows buyers to cancel the contract for nonconforming goods and to seek remedies that give them the benefit of the bargain.
Obtain cover	Buyers are allowed to substitute goods for those due under the sales contract. However, substitutes must be reasonable, acquired without delay, and obtained in good faith.
Obtain specific performance	If the goods are unique or a legal remedy is inadequate, the seller may be required to deliver the goods as identified in the contract.
Sue	Buyers are entitled to consequential and incidental damages if there is a breach of contract. They may also be able to obtain liquidated damages (damages before the breach occurs) or punitive damages.

Table 8.4

Assessment Questions

1. What is a sales contract?

2. All of the following are features of sales contracts except:
- a. Consensual.
- b. Bilateral.
- c. Cumulative.
- d. Principal.

3. What source of law governs sales contracts?
- a. Common Law.
- b. The Uniform Commercial Code.
- c. Statutory Law.
- d. Federal Law.

4. What is the definition of a good?

5. Distinguish a shipment contract from a destination contract.

6. What is a warranty in a sales contract?

7. Describe the difference between an express and implied warranty.

8. Examples of a defect in a breach of the implied warranty of merchantability, include all of the following except:

a. Design defect.
b. Manufacturing defect.
c. Inadequate instructions.
d. Product defect.

9. The following are possible remedies to buyers under the UCC:

a. Cancel the contract.
b. Obtain Cover.
c. Sue.
d. All of the above.

10. What is a breach of warranty?

Endnotes

Kubasek, N., Browne, M. N., Dhooge, L. J., Herron, D. J., Williamson, C., & Barkacs, L. L. (2015). *Dynamic business law*. McGraw-Hill Education.

Kubasek, N., Browne, M. N., Dhooge, L. J., Herron, D. J., Williamson, C., & Barkacs, L. L. (2015). *Dynamic business law*. McGraw-Hill Education.

9 Employment and Labor Law

Figure 9.1 (Credit: rawpixel/ pixabay/ Attribution 2.0 Generic (CC BY 2.0))

Chapter Outline

9.1 Employment, Worker Protection, and Immigration Law
9.2 Labor Law
9.3 Equal Opportunity in Employment

Introduction

Learning Outcome

- Analyze various laws governing employer/employee relationships.

9.1 Employment, Worker Protection, and Immigration Law

Compared to other countries in the West, stringent and extensive employee protections came fairly late to the United States. Up until 1959, for example, employers had the right to fire a worker without giving any reason. This concept, which was was known as **at-will employment**, was applicable in all states. The concept of at-will employment does, however, continue today, and all employees are considered to be at-will unless they are employed under a collective bargaining agreement, or under a contract for a set duration. Employers can still fire employees for any reason, but they cannot be fired for illegal reasons, as set out in the U.S. or state constitutions, federal law, state statutes, or public policy. In this section, some of the main employee rights and company responsibilities will be introduced.

Figure 9.2 Employees have various rights in the workplace and companies have various responsibilities toward them. (Credit: Raw Pixel/ pexels/ License: CC0)

Health and Safety

Workers have the right to be safe at work, and companies have responsibilities to employees in the event that they are harmed while undertaking work on behalf of the employer. The **Occupational Safety and Health Act**, passed in 1970, is the main legislative action that governs health and safety in the workplace. The Act established the **Occupational Safety and Health Administration** (OSHA), which is a federal agency whose role is to "assure safe and healthy working conditions for working men and women by setting and enforcing standards and by providing training, outreach, education and assistance." Private employers and federal government agencies are all covered under OSHA protection, although the self-employed and workers at state and local governments in most states are not covered. OSHA has adopted thousands of regulations to enforce the Occupational Safety and Health Act. It imposes a number of record-keeping and reporting requirements on private employers. In addition, employers are required to inform employees of their health and safety rights by posting appropriate notices in the workplace.

Type of OSHA Standard	Description	Example
Specific Duty Standards	Standards that apply to specific types of work, procedures, work conditions, and equipment	Safe handling of compressed gas cylinders

Table 9.1

General Duty Standards	Standards that apply to all employers and that impose a duty to protect workers from known hazards	Standards pertaining to ind... quality and workplace violence

Table 9.1

Workers' Compensation Acts help employees claim compensation for injuries that occur on the job. States require employers to either purchase workers' compensation insurance, or have the ability to self-insure against compensation claims. Workers' compensation insurance covers a range of different injuries, including physical injuries, mental illnesses that can be shown to be employment-related, and stress.

Under the terms of the Acts, a **Workers' Compensation Agency** is established at the state level to provide judicial and administrative services to help in the resolution of claims for compensation. In the event of a claim, a three-step process is put into place:

1. The worker files a claim with the agency.
2. The agency establishes the legitimacy of the claim.
3. If the injury is determined to be legitimate, compensation benefits are paid accordingly.

It is important to note that workers' compensation is understood to be an **exclusive remedy**. This term means that workers cannot sue the employer in court for further damages beyond that which is paid out under the compensation claim. An exception is made when the employer intentionally injures the worker, however. Furthermore, workers have the right to sue any third party involved in the cause of the injury to recover additional damages.

Case Insight

In the case Chad A. Kelley v. Marsha P. Ryan, Administrator, Ohio Bureau of Workers' Compensation, and Coca-Cola Enterprises, Chad A. Kelley attended a team-building event held by his employer, Coca-Cola, to celebrate the launch of a new product. All employees attending the event were required to canoe down a river, which Kelley, with colleagues, achieved without incident. Employees waiting on the river bank began to splash one another, and according to witnesses, Kelley said that it would take more than some splashing to get him wet. Consequently, several colleagues tried to throw Kelley into the water, which led him to sustain neck injuries. The Ohio Bureau of Workers' Compensation denied Kelley's claim for benefits, however, arguing that Kelley had instigated "horseplay" that removed the incident from the scope and course of employment. In 2009, an appellate court ruled that this conclusion was incorrect and that the employer was, in fact, responsible. Kelley was entitled to the compensation.

Fair Labor Standards Act

The Fair Labor Standards Act (FLSA) sets out provisions that delineate fair labor and unfair labor. There are three main categories covered in the Act:

1. Child labor
2. Minimum wage provisions
3. Overtime pay requirements

The FLSA prohibits oppressive **child labor** as well as the shipping of goods produced by firms that make use of

...ssive labor. The FLSA sets the minimum age for non-agricultural work as 14. However, there are some ...ons. People under the age of 14 who are classed as minors may deliver newspapers, perform ...ing or chores around the home, and can work in businesses owned by their families, as long as the ...ot deemed to be hazardous. In addition, minors may perform in television, radio, movie, or theatrical ...ons. Once an employee becomes 18, child labor regulations no longer apply.

...he terms of the FLSA, employees in covered industries, with the exception of apprentices and students, ...st be paid the federal minimum wage. Congress is responsible for reviewing the level of the minimum ... a periodic basis and raising it to compensate for increases in the cost of living caused by inflation. In 2009, Congress raised the federal minimum wage to $7.25 an hour. This increase was the first in almost a decade (although in 2014, President Obama signed an executive order that increased the minimum wage to $10.10 for those employed on new federal contracts).

FLSA also mandates that employees who work more than 40 hours in a week should receive overtime pay that is equal to at least one and one-half times their regular wage for every additional hour worked. Four categories of employees are excluded from this provision, however: executives, administrative employees, professional employees, and outside salespersons.

Family and Medical Leave Act

The Family and Medical Leave Act (FMLA), enacted in 1993, guarantees all eligible workers up to 12 weeks of unpaid leave during any 12-month period for family and medical emergencies. The FMLA applies to all public and private employers with 50 or more employees, covers employees who have worked for the employer for at least one year, and applies to employees who have worked at least 25 hours a week for each of 12 months prior to the leave. The events that qualify workers for leave are:

- The birth of a child
- The adoption of a child
- The placement of a foster child in the employee's care
- The care of a seriously ill spouse, parent, or child
- Any serious health condition that prevents the worker from being able to perform any of the essential functions of the job

Once the employee returns to work, he or she must be restored to the same or equivalent position. **Social Security** benefits also provide benefits to certain employees and their dependents. The types of benefits that fall under Social Security regulations include disability benefits, Medicare benefits, survivors' benefits, and retirement benefits.

Endi... Employment

The... are also several regulations that cover workers who are terminated or who lose their employment. Th... summarized in the following table.

...ul...n	Description

Consolidated Omnibus Budget Reconciliation Act (COBRA)	Mandates that employees who are terminated must be provided with the opportunity to continue to participate in group health insurance, so long as they agree to pay the group rate premium. The employer is required to notify employees of their COBRA rights.
Employee Retirement Income Security Act (ERISA)	This Act covers any pension plan offered by employers to their workers, and is designed to prevent abuses and fraudulent use of those plans. Under the terms of ERISA, employers are required to keep certain records pertaining to the plans, and to report on those records at regular intervals. The Act also provides for **vesting**, which occurs when an employee has a nonforfeitable right to receive pension benefits.
Unemployment compensation	Unemployment compensation programs are paid to those who become temporarily unemployed, and are funded by employers through employment taxes. Workers who quit voluntarily or who are terminated for bad conduct are not eligible for compensation. In addition, in order to qualify for the benefits, applicants must demonstrate that they are available for work.

Table 9.2

Immigration Law

There are vast areas of immigration law that are applicable to employment. The U.S. Citizenship and Immigration Service (USCIS) administers a range of different immigration programs that enable U.S. employers to employ foreign national workers. For example, under the EB-1 visa, U.S. employers can employ foreign nationals who have **extraordinary ability** for certain types of work. Under the terms of the Immigration Reform and Control Act (IRCA), employers are required to examine evidence of employees' identity and complete mandatory paperwork for each employee. There are serious financial and criminal penalties for employers who knowingly hire undocumented workers.

9.2 Labor Law

Labor relations is the general term used to describe the relationship between employers and employees, as well as governance of that relationship. It refers to the micro-level interactions that take place between workers and individual managers, as well as the macro-level relations that occur between the external institutions that are tasked with governing such relations. This understanding of labor relations acknowledges the fact that there is a plurality of interests that must be taken into account in the processes and procedures of negotiation, bargaining, and dispute settlement relating to the workplace. It also recognizes that employees and employers' representatives are fundamental to the process of industrial relations, and that the state plays a key role in the development of labor laws, the regulation of collective bargaining, and the administration of disputes. There has been considerable flux and development in the nature of U.S. labor over the past century. However, the most substantial changes have occurred since the 1950s. Changes have been particularly evident in the role that the state has been expected to play in employment relations between workers, their representatives, and their employers. This section introduces some of the key milestones in labor relations in the United States, and describes the role played by **trade unions** in governing the relationship between employers and employees.

What Is a Trade Union?

A trade union, or labor union, is an organized group of workers who come together to lobby employers about conditions affecting their work. There currently are around 60 unions representing 14 million workers across the United States. Unions are organized according to the type of work that workers do. For example, the American Federation of Teachers is the labor union for teaching personnel, while the the International Association of Fire Fighters covers fire fighters. Many unions in the United States are organized as **local unions**. This type of union is a locally (i.e., company or region) based group of workers who organize under a charter from a national union. For example, Affiliated Property Craftspersons Local 44 is the Los Angeles union of entertainment professional craftpersons, chartered under the International Alliance of Theatrical Stage Employees.

Timeline of Developments in Labor Law

- **1886.** The American Federation of Labor was formed in Columbus, Ohio. This group was a national federation of labor unions who came together to bolster their power in industrial unionism. The AFL was the largest union grouping in the United States well into the twentieth century. However, the Federation was craft-dominated, such that only craft workers like artisans and silversmiths were allowed to belong.
- **1932.** The Norris-LaGuardia Act was passed. This Act prohibited **yellow-dog contracts**, or contracts that prevented workers from joining labor unions. In addition, federal courts were barred from issuing injunctions to prevent groups of workers from engaging in boycotts, strikes, and picketing.
- **1935.** The Congress of Industrial Organizations was established. This establishment extended the union movement because it allowed semi-skilled and unskilled workers to become members.
- **1935.** The Wagner Act, or **National Labor Relations Act**, was passed. This Act is the major statute of United States labor law. The Act established that employees have the right to form, assist, and join labor organizations, to engage in collective bargaining with employers, and to engage in concerted activity to promote those rights.
- **1947.** The Labor-Management Relations Act, also known as the Taft-Hartley Act, imposed restrictions on the power of labor unions. It made changes to union election rules and outlined and provided remedies for six unfair practices by labor unions (see box below).
- **1959**. The Labor Management Reporting and Disclosure Act, or Landrum-Griffin Act, was passed, which regulates the internal affairs of trade unions, as well as their officials' relationships with employers. All union members are granted equal rights to vote for candidates, take part in membership meetings, and nominate candidates for office.
- **1988**. The Worker Adjustment and Retraining Notification (WARN) Act requires that employers with more than 100 employees give workers at least 60 days notice before engaging in layoffs or plant closings.

Amendments of the Taft-Hartley Act	Description

Table 9.3

1	Protects employees from unfair coercion by unions that could lead to discrimination against employees.
2	States that employers cannot refuse to hire prospective workers because they refuse to join a union. This amendment also grants the employer the right to sign an agreement with a union that requires the employee to join the union before the employee's 30th day of employment.
3	Unions must bargain in good faith with employers.
4	Prevents unions from engaging in secondary boycotts.
5	Prevents unions from taking advantage of either employers or members. For example, unions cannot charge members excessive membership dues or cause employers to pay for work that has not been performed.
6	Grants employers the right to free speech. Expressed opinions about labor issues do not constitute unfair labor practices, as long as the employer does not threaten to withhold benefits from, or engage in, retribution against the worker.

Table 9.3

The National Labor Relations Board

The National Labor Relations Board (NLRB) was established to administer, interpret, and enforce the terms of the National Labor Relations Act. It has jurisdiction over all workers, except for government employees and employees in the transportation industry, who are governed under a separate statute (The Railway Labor Act). Other workers not covered by the NLRB include agricultural workers, confidential employees (employees who develop or present management's position or who have access to confidential information related to bargaining employees), independent contractors, and those employed by a spouse or a parent. The NLRB has three main functions:

1. To monitor the conduct of unions and employers during elections to determine whether employees wish to be represented by a union
2. To remedy and prevent unfair labor practices by unions or employers
3. To establish rules interpreting the NLRA

Figure 9.3 Under the terms of the National Labor Relations Act, employees have the right to strike as part of their efforts to secure better working conditions. (Credit: Geralt/ pixabay/ License: CC0)

Organizing a Union

For a union to be formed and organized, the union must identify an **appropriate bargaining unit.** This term is used to describe the group of workers that the union is looking to represent. Under the terms of the **inaccessibility exception,** employees and union officials have the right to engage in union solicitation on the firm's property if they cannot otherwise access employees to communicate with them. The next stage is to run an election. There are three types of elections:

- **Consent election.** This election is held when there are not any substantial issues under dispute between the union and the employer. Both parties agree to waive the pre-election hearing.
- **Contest election**. This election is for a union that is contested by the employer. The NLRB is required to supervise this kind of election.
- A **decertification election** is held when employees indicate that they wish to vote out the union or join another.

In order to try to bolster their power, elected unions often attempt to install a **union security agreement.** This agreement pertains to the extent to which the union can demand that employees join the union, and whether the employer will be required to collect fees and dues on behalf of the union. A **closed shop** is a workplace where union membership is a requirement for employment. A **union shop** is a place of employment where the employee is required to join the union within a specified number of days after being hired. An **agency shop** is a workplace that does not require the employee to join the union, but where agency fees to the union must be paid. Union security agreements are the outcome of collective bargaining agreements.

Collective Bargaining

Collective bargaining involves the union and the employer negotiating contract terms. The outcome is known as a **collective bargaining agreement.** The types of terms that are usually negotiated are wages and salaries, hours, and the terms and conditions of employment. If union members dispute working conditions, unfair labor practices, or economic benefits, they have the right to participate in a cessation of work activities, known as a **strike**. There is a mandatory cooling off period of sixty days before a strike can commence. Some collective bargaining agreements include no-strike clauses. Although strikes are permitted according to the NRLA, some strikes are illegal:

- Violent strikes
- Sit-down strikes
- Wildcat (unauthorized) strikes
- Intermittent, or partial strikes

In addition to striking, union members have the right to picket. This process involves walking in front of the employer's premises with signs that advertise the strike and the union's demands. Picketing is lawful as long as it does not:

- Involve violence
- Prevent customers from entering the premises
- Prevent non-striking workers from entering the premises
- Prevent the business from receiving deliveries or pickups

Secondary boycott picketing occurs when the union pickets the employer's customers or suppliers. This type of picketing is legal if it is product picketing, but illegal if the picket is directed against a neutral business.

9.3 Equal Opportunity in Employment

A Landmark Case

In 1982, the financial services company Price Waterhouse announced a vacancy for the position of partner. Ann Hopkins, an employee of the company at the time, applied, but after an assessment, was passed over. Hopkins sued the company, arguing that she had billed more than $34 million in consulting contracts for the firm, far more than any of the other 87 candidates, who were all male. In rejecting her application, the partners at the company argued that Hopkins was "too macho" and that she should "walk more femininely, talk more femininely, dress more femininely, wear makeup, have her hair styled and wear jewelry." In the landmark legal suit that followed, Hopkins was awarded $371,000 in back pay, and Price Waterhouse was forced to make her a partner.

Laws Governing Equal Opportunity in Employment

Employees are protected in the workplace by a number of laws enacted at both the federal and state levels. Federal laws are usually considered to be the minimum level of protection, and state laws can provide employees with more, but not less, protection. In this section, the major laws pertaining to equal opportunity are discussed.

Civil Rights Act of 1964 – Title VII (Amended By the Civil Rights Act of 1991)

The Civil Rights Act provides broad provisions pertaining to citizens' civil rights. Title VII of the Civil Rights Act deals with discrimination in employment. It bans employers from discriminating against employees in their hiring, firing, and promotion practices on the basis of sex, national origin, color, religion, or race. All employers who are engaged in commercial activity and who employ 15 or more employees for 20 consecutive weeks in a year are covered by the Act. The Act also sets out the two main ways in which discrimination can be proven: disparate treatment and disparate impact.

Disparate treatment means that the employee believes that he or she has been discriminated against on the basis of one of the protected classes set out in the CRA. Proving that the employer engaged in disparate treatment is a three-step process:

1. The employee (plaintiff) is required to demonstrate a **prima facie** (accepted as correct unless proven otherwise) case of discrimination.
2. The employer (defendant) must show legitimate, non-discriminatory business reasons for undertaking the action.
3. The employee must demonstrate that the reason given by the employer is a mere pretext.

A trier of fact, usually a jury, will use the evidence presented to determine whether discrimination did in fact occur. If the jury finds for the employee-plaintiff, damages can be awarded, such as what occurred in the landmark Ann Hopkins case, described in the opening box. If the jury finds for the employer-defendant, no damages are assessed.

Damages Permissible Under Title VII of the CRA
Up to two years of back pay
Compensatory damages
Punitive damages
Remedial seniority
Costs (e.g., attorney fees and court costs)
Court orders (e.g., reinstatement)

Table 9.4

Disparate impact cases are cases of unintentional discrimination. This type of case occurs when the employer engages in a practice that has a disproportionately injurious impact on a protected class. Disparate impact cases are difficult to prove. The burden of responsibility is on the employee-plaintiff to statistically establish that the action impacts the protected class. The defendant can avoid liability by demonstrating that the practice is a business responsibility. The burden of proof then shifts to the employee to prove that the alleged business necessity is a mere pretext. These steps were established in Griggs v. Duke Power Co. Duke Power required all job applicants to have a high school diploma and to reach a certain minimum score on a professional intelligence test. Willie Griggs, the plaintiff, established that the rule was racially discriminatory because only 12 percent of black men in the state had high school diplomas (compared to 34 percent of white men), and only 6 percent of blacks had passed similar intelligence tests, compared to 58 percent of whites. Duke Power tried to argue that the provisions were necessary to upgrade the quality of the workforce, but the court did not agree that this defense was an adequate business-related justification, and the plaintiff was successful.

Figure 9.4 Employees are protected against discrimination by employers by a number of laws enacted at both the federal and state level. (Credit: Wokandapix/ pixabay/ License: CC0)

Sexual harassment is also protected under Title VII. This type of harassment is defined as unwelcome sexual advances, requests for sexual favors, and other verbal or physical conduct of a sexual nature. Two types of sexual harassment are recognized. **Quid pro quo** occurs when a manager makes a sexual demand on a worker, and this demand is perceived as a condition of employment. Actions that create a **hostile work environment** are another type of sexual harassment. These issues have been used in cases of discrimination based on race and religion as well as sex. Since the 1997 case Oncale v. Sundowner Offshore Services Inc., it has been established that sexual harassment undertaken by a member of one sex against a member of the same sex is actionable under Title VII. In some limited circumstances, employers may also be liable for harassment of employees by non-employees, e.g., customers. The employer is liable if it does nothing to prevent and remedy harassment targeted at one of its employees. The **Pregnancy Discrimination Act** of 1987 expanded the definition of sex discrimination to include discrimination based on pregnancy, childbirth, or medical conditions related to the same.

Defenses to Title VII Claims

Defense	Description

Table 9.5

The Bona Fide Occupational Qualification Defense (BFOQ)	Using this defense, the employer can discriminate if it is deemed to be necessary for the performance of the job. Necessity, however, must be determined on the basis of actual qualifications, rather than stereotypes about the abilities of a certain class. For example, an employer is not expected to hire a man as a model for women's clothes. Hires on the basis of sexual privacy are covered under BFOQ. However, there are no BFOQs for discrimination on the basis of race or color.
The Merit Defense	This defense is used when decisions pertaining to hiring or promotion are made on the basis of the results of test scores. However, tests must be validated in accordance with professional standards and must be manifestly related to job performance.
The Seniority Defense System	This defense system occurs when employees are given preferential treatment because of their length of tenure. As long as the system does not have its genesis in discrimination, and is not used to discriminate and applies to all persons equally, it is lawful.

Table 9.5

The Equal Pay Act

The Equal Pay Act (EPA) is a United States federal law that seeks to equalize the salaries and wages paid to employed women with the levels paid to men for work of an equal nature and quantity. The Act amended the Fair Labor Standard Act of 1938 and was a key element of President F. Kennedy's New Frontier program. Under the terms of the EPA, women and men performing jobs that demand "equal skill, effort, and responsibility, and which are performed under similar working conditions" must be paid the same. The Act protects the rights of both sexes. An individual who seeks to establish a case under the Act must demonstrate that:

1. An employer pays one sex more than another
2. Both sexes perform an equal amount of work that demands equal levels of skill, effort and responsibility
3. Working conditions for both sexes are equivalent

An employer that is accused of discrimination under the EPA can present one of four **affirmative defenses**. An employer may legally pay employees of one sex more than another sex if wages are based on a system of seniority, a system of merit, a system that distinguishes payment on the basis of quality and quantity of production (e.g., certain piece rates), or if payment is differentiated on "any other factor other than sex." Of these four defenses, the "factor other than sex" defense has been invoked most frequently and has been the subject of intense debate and controversy. Critics have argued that this defense enables employers to fabricate other reasons for the wage gap.

Americans with Disabilities Act

The Americans with Disabilities Act (ADA) prevents employers from discriminating against workers on the basis of their physical or mental disabilities. In addition, employers are required to make reasonable accommodations to known disabilities, as long as such accommodations do not impose an undue burden on the business. To bring a successful ADA claim, the plaintiff is required to demonstrate that he or she:

- Has a disability
- Suffered an adverse employment decision because of that disability

- Was otherwise qualified for the position

ADA is enforced in a similar way to Title VII, and remedies for ADA violations are also similar.

Age Discrimination Act

Passed in 1967, this Act prohibits employers from making discriminatory employment decisions against people age 40 or older. This Act applies to all employers with 20 or more employees.

Assessment Questions

1. What does At-Will Employment mean?

2. Employers are required provide a work environment that is safe and healthy for their employees by which law?

a. FLSA.
b. WCA.
c. OHSA.
d. FMLA.

3. How many weeks of unpaid leave does the Family Medical Leave Act guarantee to eligible workers?

a. 12.
b. 16.
c. 25.
d. 40.

4. What regulation protects employees who are terminated from their employment?

a. COBRA.
b. ERISA.
c. Unemployment Compensation.
d. All of the above.

5. The Fair Labor Standards Act (FLSA) covers which category?

a. Child Labor.
b. Minimum wage.
c. Overtime pay.
d. All of the above.

6. Explain the term labor relations.

7. What is a trade union?

8. What is the function of the National Labor Relations Board?

a. To monitor the conduct of the unions and employers during union elections.
b. To remedy and prevent unfair labor practices by unions or employers.
c. To establish rules interpreting the NLRA.
d. All of the above.

9. ____ is a place of employment where the employee is required to join the union within a specified number of days after being hired.

a. A closed shop.
b. A union shop.
c. An agency shop.
d. A secure shop.

10. Which of the following practices are illegal?

a. Picketing.
b. No strike clause.
c. Sit-Down strike.
d. A secure shop.

11. Explain Title VII of the Civil Rights Act of 1964.

12. How do you prove a disparate impact case?

13. The following is valid defense under Title VII:

a. Quid Pro Quo.
b. No Merit Defense.
c. BFOQ
d. All of the above.

14. To bring a successful claim under the Americans with Disability Act ("ADA"), the plaintiff must prove all of the following except:

a. He or she suffered an adverse employment decision because of a disability.
b. The disability was not a mental disability.
c. He or she was qualified for a position.
d. He or she has a disability.

15. The Age Discrimination Act only applies to employers with 20 or more employees.

a. True.
b. False.

Endnotes

Blanpain, R., & Bisom-Rapp, S. (2014). *Global Workplace: International and Comparative Employment Law Cases and Materials*. Wolters Kluwer Law & Business.

Cheeseman, H. (2016). *Business Law*. Boston: Pearson Education.

Robinson, T. (2011). "The Top 10 Bizarre Workers' Comp Cases for 2010." LexisNexis Legal NewsRoom. Retrieved from: https://www.lexisnexis.com/legalnewsroom/workers-compensation/b/workers-compensation-law-blog/posts/the-top-10-bizarre-workers-comp-cases-for-2010

Cheeseman, H. (2016). *Business Law*. Boston: Pearson Education.

Feldacker, B. S., & Hayes, M. J. (2014). *Labor guide to labor law*. Ithaca: Cornell University Press.

Rutherglen, G. (2016). Employment Discrimination Law, Visions of Equality in Theory and Doctrine. West Academic.

Woloch, N. (2018). Because of Sex: One Law, Ten Cases, and Fifty Years That Changed American Women's Lives at Work by Gillian Thomas. Labor: Studies in Working-Class History, 15(1), 128–129.

10 Government Regulation

Figure 10.1 (Credit: JamesDeMers/ pixabay/ Attribution 2.0 Generic (CC BY 2.0))

Chapter Outline

10.1 Administrative Law
10.2 Regulatory Agencies

Introduction

Learning Outcome

- Define the role of administrative bodies and regulation in the governmental rulemaking process.

10.1 Administrative Law

Administrative law is also referred to as **regulatory** and **public law**. It is the law that is related to administrative agencies. Administrative agencies are established by statutes and governed by rules, regulations and orders, court decisions, judicial orders, and decisions.

Agencies are created by federal or state governments to carry out certain goals or purposes. Federal agencies are created by an act of Congress. Congress writes out a law called an **organic statute** that lays out the purpose and structure of the agency. The agency is charged with carrying out that purpose, as described by Congress. **Organic statutes** are utilized to create administrative agencies, as well as to define their responsibilities and authority.

Figure 10.2 Both federal and state legislators create agencies to fulfill a specific purpose, usually related to protecting the public from a potential threat. (Credit: kbhall17/ pixabay/ License: CC0)

Industrialization

Administrative agencies have been around almost since the founding of the United States. However, **industrialization** had a big impact on the development of administrative laws. As people moved from farms and rural areas to cities to find work and raise families, the economy changed. It became more complex. As a result of this economic change, the government saw a need to expand its regulation to protect and support the public. In the 20th century, the number of agencies expanded very quickly with the addition of the Food and Drug Administration (FDA) to regulate food and medication, the Federal Trade Commission (FTC) to regulate trade, and the Federal Reserve System (FRS) to regulate banks. These are just a few of the agencies created to regulate industries. Ultimately, this expansion occurred in response to the complexity of the economy.

Figure 10.3 Industrialization increased the number of administrative agencies in the United States. (Credit: Chevanon Photography/ pexels/ License: CC0)

Everyday Impact

Administrative law impacts the public on a daily basis. Administrative law is basically the delegated power granted to administrative agencies to carry out specific functions. Government agencies endeavor to protect the rights of citizens, corporations, and any other entity through administrative laws. Administrative agencies were developed to protect consumers and the community. As a result, they are present in all aspects of life, including medicine, food, environment, and trade.

One well-known federal agency is the Food and Drug Administration (FDA). The FDA was created to protect the public's health. The agency's responsibilities are very broad. The agency fulfills its role by ensuring the safety and effectiveness of drugs consumed by people and animals, biological products, medical devices, food, and cosmetics. Specifically, the FDA regulates the things that the public consumes, including supplements, infant formula, bottled water, food additives, eggs, some meat, and other food products. The FDA also regulates biological items and medical devices, including vaccines, cellular therapy products, surgical implants, and dental devices. This federal agency began in 1906 with the passing of the Pure Food and Drugs Act.

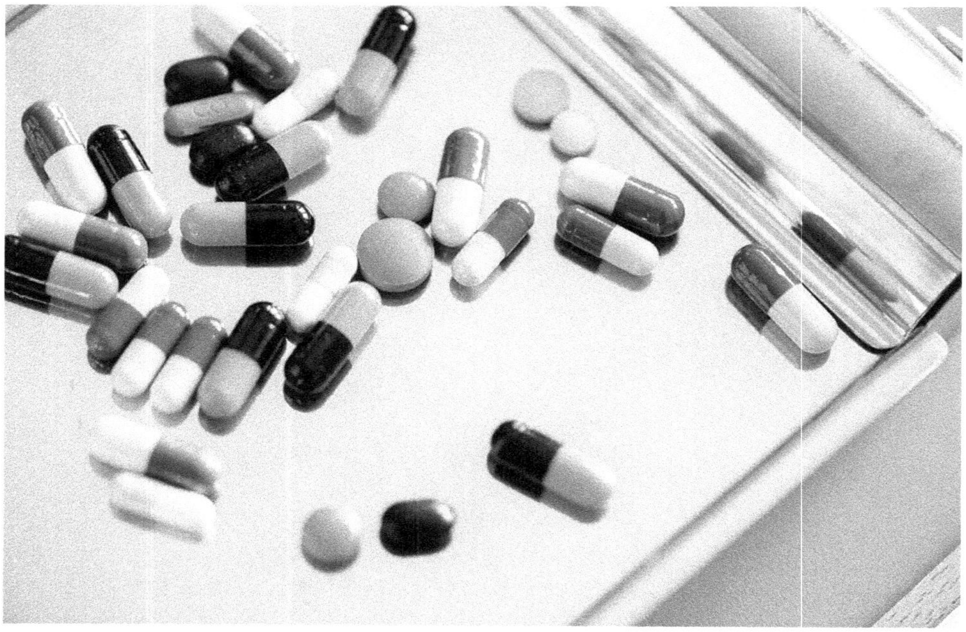

Figure 10.4 The Food and Drug Administration (FDA) oversees the safety and effectiveness of medication. (Credit: Rawpixel/ pexels/ License: CC0)

EpiPens are automatic injection devices that deliver lifesaving medication that can save an individual in the event of exposure to an allergen, like a bee sting or peanuts. The United States faced a shortage of EpiPens, so in 2018, the FDA took action to address this issue. The FDA approved the extension of EpiPen expiration dates for four months on specific lots of the EpiPen. This extension impacted both the public and the organization that produces EpiPens. In the same year, the FDA approved the first generic EpiPen. The new generic version will be produced by a pharmaceutical company that has not previously produced the EpiPen. These two actions impact consumers by increasing the supply of lifesaving EpiPens.

Another well-known agency is the Federal Trade Commission (FTC). The FTC was formed in 1914 when President Woodrow Wilson signed the Federal Trade Commission Act into law. The goal of the agency is to protect the consumer, encourage business competition, and further the interests of consumers by encouraging innovation. The FTC works within the United States as well as internationally to protect consumers and encourage competition. The agency fulfills this role by developing policies, partnering with law enforcement to ensure consumer protection, and helping to ensure that markets are open and free. For instance, management and enforcement of the Do Not Call List is part of the FTC's consumer protection goals.

The FTC protects consumers from unfair or misleading practices. Phone scams are a common issue. Scammers go to great lengths to trick the public into donating to false charities, providing personal information, or giving access to financial information. The FTC is aware of these issues and has put rules in place to punish scammers and educate the public. The FTC created a phone scammer reporting process to help collect information about scammers so that they can be prosecuted. The agency also collects information about scammers and creates educational materials for the public. These materials are designed to help consumers identify possible phone scammers, avoid their tactics, and report their activities.

A complete list of U.S. government agencies can be found at https://www.usa.gov/federal-agencies/a (https://www.usa.gov/federal-agencies/a) .

10.2 Regulatory Agencies

The power of administrative agencies comes from the executive branch of the government. Congress passes laws to carry out specific **directives**. The passing of these laws often creates a need for a government agency that will implement and carry out these laws. The government is not able to perform the work itself or manage the employees who will do the work. Instead, it creates agencies to do this. Assigning this authority to agencies is called **delegation**. The agencies have focus and expertise in their specific area of authority. However, it is important to note that Congress gives these agencies just enough power to fulfill their responsibilities.

Although administrative agencies are created by Congress, most administrative agencies are part of the executive branch of the government. The executive branch of government of the United States is headed by the president of the United States. Administrative agencies are created to enforce and administer laws, and the executive branch was created to oversee administrative agencies. Administrative agencies conduct exams and investigations of the entities they regulate. As a result of being part of the executive branch of government, the leaders of administrative agencies are generally appointed by the executive branch.

Figure 10.5 Most administrative agencies are housed in the executive branch. The president of the United States appoints leaders to administrative agencies. (Credit: Aaron Kittredge/ pexels/ License: CC0)

Administrative agencies also have responsibilities that mirror the responsibilities of the judicial branch of government. Administrative law judges (ALJ) have two primary duties. First, they oversee procedural aspects, like depositions of witnesses related to a case. They have the ability to review rules and statutes and review decisions related to their agencies. They also determine the facts and then make a judgment related to whether or not the agency's rules were broken. They act like a trial judge in a court, but their jurisdiction is limited to evaluating if rules established by certain government agencies were violated. They can award money, other benefits, and punish those found guilty of violating the rules.

Federal Agencies

Well-known federal agencies include the Federal Bureau of Investigations (FBI), Environmental Protection Agency (EPA), Food and Drug Administration (FDA), Federal Trade Commission (FTC), Federal Election Commission (FEC), and the National Labor Relations Board (NLRB). These agencies were created to serve specific purposes. For instance, the FBI was created to investigate federal crimes. A federal crime is one that violates federal criminal law, rather than a state's criminal law. The EPA was created to combine federal functions that were instituted protect the environment. The NLRB was created to carry out the National Labor Relations Act of 1935.

The goal of federal agencies is to protect the public. The EPA was created in response to concerns about the dumping of toxic chemicals in waterways and about air pollution. It began when the Cuyahoga River in Ohio burst into flames without warning. President Richard Nixon presented a plan to reduce pollution from cars, end the dumping of pollutants into waterways, tax businesses for some environmentally unfriendly practices, and reduce pollution in other ways. The EPA was created by Congress in response to these environmental concerns and President Richard Nixon's plan. It is given the authority and responsibility to protect the environment from businesses, so that the people can enjoy a clean and safe environment.

As mentioned in the previous section, the Federal Trade Commission (FTC) was created to protect the consumer. It investigates and addresses activities that limit competition between businesses. The organization enforces **antitrust laws** that prevent one organization from restraining competition or seeking to maintain full control over a market. In December of 2006, the FTC ruled on the merger of America Online, Inc. (AOL) and Time Warner, Inc. The FTC decided that the joining of these two companies would limit the ability of other organizations to compete in the cable internet marketplace. The FTC ordered the merged company, AOL Time Warner, to do certain things that permitted competitors to engage, including opening its system to competitors' internet services and not interfering with the transmission signal being passed through the system. Doing so prevented the large company from shutting out its competitors. These are just a few examples of administrative agencies that were created to protect the community from business activities that could negatively impact the environment or the consumer.

Figure 10.6 Although administrative agencies have a great deal of power, they are bound by the concept of due process at is described in the U.S. Constitution. (Credit: wynpnt/ pixabay/ License: CC0)

Agency Structure

Administrative agencies are made up of experts, and they are trusted by Congress to identify the agency structure that best serves their specific goals. Thus, each agency is structured differently.

The FTC is a well-known agency and is organized into bureaus. Each bureau is focused on an agency goal. The three bureaus are consumer protection, competition, and economics. The Bureau of Consumer Protection focuses on unfair and deceptive business practices by encouraging consumers to voice complaints, investigate, and file lawsuits against companies. It also develops rules to maintain fair practices and educates consumers and businesses about rights and responsibilities. The Bureau of Competition focuses on antitrust laws and, by doing so, supports lower prices and choices for the consumer. And, lastly, the Bureau of Economics concentrates on consumer protection investigation, rulemaking, and the economic impact of government regulations on businesses and consumers.

Administrative Procedure Act (APA)

These agencies are not unrestrained in their operations. First, there are due process requirements created in the Constitution. Rules must be reasonable and based on facts. Second, rules cannot violate anyone's constitutional rights or civil liberties. Third, there must be an opportunity for the public to voice its support, or lack of support, for a rule. In 1946, the **Administrative Procedure Act (APA)** was enacted. Under the APA, agencies must follow certain procedures to make their rules enforceable statutes. The Act set up a full system for the execution of administrative law by administrative agencies for the federal government. Although agencies have power, government agencies must still act within the structures in place, including the Constitution, span of authority, statutory limitations, and other restrictions. The APA outlines roles, powers, and procedures of agencies. It organizes administrative functions into rulemaking and adjudication.

Assessment Questions

1. What is administrative law?

2. Administrative agencies are created by:

a. The president.
b. The judicial branch.
c. The Constitution.
d. Congress.

3. The FDA stands for:

a. The First Drug Administration.
b. The Federal Drug Administration.
c. The Food and Drug Administration.
d. The Food and Diet Administration.

4. Explain the goal of the Federal Trade Commission.

5. How does the FDA fulfill its role?

6. Who appoints leaders to run administrative agencies?

a. The President.
b. Congress.
c. The judges.
d. None of these are correct.

7. The process of assigning authority to administrative agencies is called:

a. An assignment.
b. A directive.
c. A passing.
d. A delegation.

8. What's the role of an Administrative Law Judge (ALJ)?

9. The Bureau of Economics concentrates on all but the following:

a. Consumer protection investigation.
b. Rulemaking.
c. Lower prices for consumers.
d. Economic impact of government regulation.

10. Explain the purpose of the Administrative Procedure Act ("APA").

Endnotes

FTC Approves AOL/Time Warner Merger with Conditions. (December 14, 2000). *Federal Trade Commission.* Retrieved from: https://www.ftc.gov/news-events/press-releases/2000/12/ftc-approves-aoltime-warner-merger-conditions.

Johnson, C. Y., & McGinley, L. (August 16, 2018). "FDA Approves First Generic Version of EpiPen." *The*

Washington Post. Retrieved from: https://www.washingtonpost.com/news/to-your-health/wp/2018/08/16/fda-approves-first-generic-version-of-epipen/?utm_term=.04ace0ebeaa6.

Phone Scams. Retrieved from: https://www.consumer.ftc.gov/articles/0076-phone-scams.

The Origins of EPA. *EPA: United States Environmental Protection Agency.* Retrieved from: https://www.epa.gov/history/origins-epa.

What is Administrative Law? *Tech Policy Lab, University of Washington.* Retrieved from: https://www.youtube.com/watch?v=ow5hZmU7Yfw.

Aguirre, D., & Von Post, R. (December 05, 2013). "Culture's Critical Role in Change Management." *Strategy Business*. Retrieved from: https://www.strategy-business.com/blog/Cultures-Critical-Role-in-Change-Management?gko=a3f98.

Mungei, V., et al. (February 22, 2012). "The Role of Education and Training to the Success of TQM Implementation." *Teamwork and Employee Empowerment.* Retrieved from: http://tqmgroups.blogspot.com/p/role-of-education-and-training-to.html.

Napierala, B. (June 22, 2012). "Five Important Factors in Total Quality Management." *Five Important Factors in Total Quality Management.* Retrieved from: http://aboutthree.com/blog/five-important-factors-in-total-quality-management/.

Stid, D., & Kramer, K. (N.d). "The Effective Organization: Five Questions to Translate Leadership into Strong Management." *The Bridgespan Group.* Retrieved from: https://www.bridgespan.org/insights/library/organizational-effectiveness/the-effective-organization-five-questions.

11 Antitrust Law

Figure 11.1 (Credit: witwiccan/ pixabay/ Attribution 2.0 Generic (CC BY 2.0))

Chapter Outline

11.1 History of Antitrust Law
11.2 Antitrust Laws

Introduction

Learning Outcome

- Analyze the tenets of antitrust laws in the United States.

11.1 History of Antitrust Law

What if the two largest manufacturers of soft drinks, Coca Cola Co. and PepsiCo, merged? It is likely that the mega-company that resulted would dominate the soft drink industry, squeezing out all of the other smaller competitors.

Figure 11.2 Without antitrust laws, the shelves would have fewer products for consumers to choose from. Image: Beverages, Bottles, Shelf. (Credit: igorovsyannyko/ pixabay/ License: CC0)

In the late 1800s, concern over this kind of merger, as well as other attempts by large companies to create monopolies or to control the market, led state and federal lawmakers to take steps to reduce the risks associated with this type of practice.

Business Trusts

During the late 1800s, the United States became concerned about the development of corporate monopolies dominating the manufacturing and mining industries (Jurist, n.d.). The end of the Civil War marked the beginning of large advances in industrialization. Many large companies formed, especially in the oil and steel industries, which were two industries that the country was beginning to heavily rely on. Manufacturing and distributing companies grew at a fast pace in a wide variety of industries, ranging from sugar to beef to tobacco (West, n.d.). The problem was that the growth occurred so rapidly that supply exceeded demand. This outcome increased competition, and many companies sought to reduce the number of competitors through forms of **restraint of trade** such as price-fixing, monopolies, and mergers (West, n.d.).

Figure 11.3 The oil industry expanded quicker than demand, causing companies to try to remove competition. (Credit: 15299/ pixabay/ License: CC0)

Some of the competitors were larger and more powerful than others, and they sought to limit the competition in the market by taking steps to reduce the number of smaller companies who were trying to compete with them (Federal Trade Commission, n.d.). Some of the larger companies banded together to create **business trusts**. A business trust is a trust agreement that allows businesses to maintain profits as beneficiaries, but legal ownership and management of the company's property is maintained through the power of trustees (West, n.d.). These trusts allowed businesses that were members of the trust to grow larger, as they cooperated with one another and shut out other competitors (West, n.d.).

Unfair Business Practices

Companies tried to create situations that would drive some competitors out of business while solidifying their own share of the market. This effort resulted in mergers and consolidation practices that placed the largest share of the industries under the control of just a few, thereby increasing their power. Since the trusts were able to fix prices and could afford to take some losses, they would drive prices down until competitors were forced out of business because they could not afford to operate at the lower rates (West. n.d.).

The markets began to consolidate under just a few companies because the smaller competitors continued to go out of business. The smaller competitors could not compete with the pricing and other practices that the trusts allowed the cooperative businesses to maintain. This design restricted free trade practices for both businesses and consumers. The few businesses in the trust, in turn, became more powerful, thus prompting the government to look for measures to control the situation (Federal Trade Commission, n.d.). The government determined that laws needed to be created to prevent this form of trade restriction.

Rule of Reason

Unfair business practices did not reside solely with business trusts. Issues also occurred in agreements between competitors, contracts entered into between sellers and buyers, and practices that created or maintained cartels, monopolies, and mergers (West, n.d.). There were no specific laws that regulated these practices, so the courts were not entirely sure how to deal with them. Initially, courts seemed to swing both ways, both accepting and condemning certain forms of restraint of trade. Rulings were not consistent from state to state, and guidelines needed to be established. The guiding condition seemed to be whether or not the restraints prevented other merchants from entering the market (West, n.d.).

The courts used the **rule of reason** as the standard. The rule of reason explored the goal of the contract, which was considered either naked restraint or ancillary restraint. **Naked restraint** occurs as contracts promote a general restraint of competition. If the restraint was created with a goal of long-term impact without boundaries, it was considered to be a naked restraint (West, nd.). **Ancillary restraint** occurs as the restriction is limited in time and geography (West, n.d.). With ancillary restraint, the restraint would be short-term and limited in scope. The courts tended to frown upon naked restraint, but were less consistent with ancillary restraint. Initially, there did not seem to be a comprehensive common law applied similarly from state to state (West, n.d.). This problem was concerning enough to warrant a solution, and in 1890, the first antitrust law was enacted (Jurist, n.d.).

Antitrust Laws

Antitrust laws regulate economic competition in an effort to maintain fair trade practices (West, n.d.). They were created to prevent the restraints on trade created by trusts and other large company practices. These restraints often resulted in price-fixing, control of production, and control of geographical markets (Jurist, n.d.). Many states recognized these outcomes as a threat to fair business practices. The federal government also recognized this issue and developed antitrust laws in 1887 as a result of a Standard Oil trust that was formed. The Standard Oil Trust occurred as oil companies transferred their stocks to a trustee to create a more powerful block of oil companies that prevented other oil companies from effectively competing with them (West, n.d.).

The first antitrust law created was the Sherman Antitrust Act in 1890, which became the basis for subsequent antitrust laws (Jurist, 2013). The Sherman Act was a good start, but it was not comprehensive enough to prevent trusts, and large companies continued to exert strong control over industries. At the turn of the century, a few large companies controlled almost half of all of the nation's manufacturing assets (West, n.d.). It became evident that more legislation was necessary. President Theodore Roosevelt dubbed himself a "trustbuster," and he began a campaign to create more effective legal endeavors (West, n.d.). Additional antitrust acts were passed in 1914, including the Clayton Act and the Federal Trade Commission Act. These acts are still in effect, and since 1914, they have been amended by Congress to continue to expand upon and solidify the coverage. It is estimated that antitrust laws save consumers millions of dollars a year, as they prohibit business practices that unfairly raise prices on goods and services (United States Department of Justice, n.d.).

Conclusion

The original purpose of antitrust legislation, i.e., to foster competition that results in lower prices, more products, and more equal distribution of wealth between producers, remains relevant today (West, n.d.). Yet, large companies still seek advantages in trade and work to put competitors out of business. It is important to

This OpenStax book is available for free at http://cnx.org/content/col30149/1.5

maintain unrestrained trade and prevent the few from having too much power over the many.

Sources

Federal Trade Commission (n.d.). The antitrust laws. Retrieved from: https://www.ftc.gov/tips-advice/competition-guidance/guide-antitrust-laws/antitrust-laws.

Jurist (2013). History of antitrust laws. Retrieved from: https://www.jurist.org/archives/feature/a-history-and-the-main-acts/.

United States Department of Justice (n.d.). Antitrust laws and you. Retrieved from: https://www.justice.gov/atr/antitrust-laws-and-you.

West's Encyclopedia of American Law (n.d.). Antitrust law. Retrieved from: >http://iris.nyit.edu/~shartman/mba0101/trust.htm.

11.2 Antitrust Laws

Antitrust legislation was designed to prevent unfair restrictions on trade and to maintain equal opportunity for trade for businesses and consumers alike. Throughout the history of antitrust laws, legislation has become more comprehensive and structured to keep up with the business practices of larger corporations that continue to seek advantages and control through trade practices.

What Do Antitrust Laws Do?

Antitrust laws were created to prevent unlawful mergers and business practices that could lead to restraint of trade by others (Federal Trade Commission, n.d.). The laws themselves are somewhat general to allow the courts the ability to make decisions on these practices, based on changing times and markets (Federal Trade Commission, n.d.). The three main antitrust laws that are in effect have been in effect for over 100 years and through many changes in society—from an industrial age to a technological age, and the changing markets they represent. The federal government created and enforces these three main antitrust laws:

- The Sherman Antitrust Act
- The Clayton Act
- The Federal Trade Commission Act

Each state has its own antitrust laws that pertain to trade practices within each separate state, but federal laws are able to reach beyond the states to interstate trade.

The Sherman Antitrust Act

The Sherman Act was passed in 1890 and focused on trade restraints that were considered unreasonable (Federal Trade Commission, n.d.). This Act did not prohibit all forms of trade restraint, since the courts did not see temporary limited restraints as an issue at the time. A partnership agreement that limited trade to certain areas for certain partners was considered acceptable. The courts deemed some trade restrictions as unreasonable, such as price fixing (Federal Trade Commission, n.d.). In some cases, the violation was so apparent that the violation was considered **prima facie**, or so evident that it automatically satisfied the unreasonable standard (Jurist, 2013).

The Sherman Act prohibits all contracts and interactions that unreasonably restrain foreign trade and trade between states (United States Department of Justice, n.d.). This prohibition does not mean that companies cannot lower prices on goods in an effort to outsell the competition. Doing so would be considered fair competition and trade. However, when a company is able to suppress the ability of others to compete through some intentional unfair business practice, such as forming agreements with competitors to set prices, it is considered a violation.

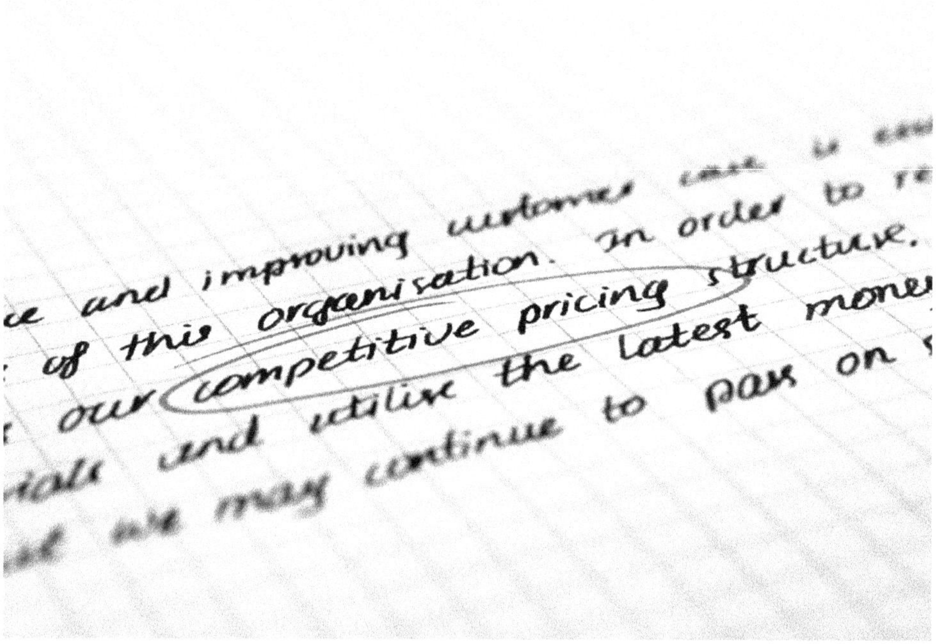

Figure 11.4 Competitive pricing is a normal part of business until it involves unfair trade practices. (Credit: pixabay/ pexels/ CC0)

The Act is a criminal statute, meaning that violation of this Act would result in criminal penalties. Mergers or other actions that would create agreements to fix prices or bids or allocate customers are considered criminal felonies (The United States Department of Justice, n.d.). Violations of the Sherman Act could lead to penalties of up to $100 million for larger corporations and up to $1 million for individuals (Federal Trade Commission, n.d.). Those convicted could also face up to 10 years in prison. If the amount gained by the conspirators, or the amount lost by the victims of the crime, is over $100 million, the fine could be increased to twice the amount gained by the conspirators or lost by the victims—whichever is greater (Federal Trade Commission, n.d.).

The Sherman Act did have limitations. It did not provide clear and specific language, which left the courts to make decisions on a case-by-case basis, without any consistent **precedent** on which to rely (West, n.d.). Precedent occurs as courts make rulings in certain cases, and those rulings are followed in subsequent cases. This lack of precedent left many larger companies in control of their restraint of trade practices, and new legislation seemed necessary.

The Clayton Act

The Clayton Act was passed in 1914. The Clayton Act is a civil statute rather than a criminal statute, meaning that it carries civil penalties rather than prison sentences (United States Department of Justice, n.d.). It primarily focuses on unfair mergers and acquisitions (Jurist, 2013). This Act sought to create more specific language to help the courts reduce unfair trade practices. As such, it established four acts as illegal, but not criminal, meaning that they would be tried as civil matters. The four acts are (West, n.d.):

- Price discrimination, which occurs as the same product is sold to different buyers at different prices
- Exclusive dealing contracts, which require buyers to purchase only from one business and not competitors
- Corporate mergers, which result in the acquisition of competing companies
- Interlocking directorates, which are boards of competing companies with common members sitting on each of the boards

The four acts would only be considered illegal when they create monopolies or substantially lessen competition (West, n.d.). Unions were excluded from mention in the Clayton Act, as Congress did not wish to treat human labor as a commodity (West, n.d.). This Act was still broad enough to rely on the courts for interpretation and decisions on a case-by-case basis.

The Clayton Act was amended in 1976 to require companies planning larger mergers and acquisitions to notify the government in advance and seek authorization (Federal Trade Commission, n.d.). This amendment also provides individuals who are victims of these practices with the ability to sue for triple damages after harm is established (Federal Trade Commission, n.d.).

The Federal Trade Commission Act

The Federal Trade Commission Act (FTC Act), also passed in 1914, focuses on unfair methods of competition and deceptive acts or practices that impact commerce (West, n.d.). All acts that violate the Sherman Act also violate the FTC Act (Federal Trade Commission, n.d.). The FTC Act works to fill in the gaps of the unfair practices by condemning all anticompetitive behaviors not otherwise covered in the other federal antitrust laws (West, n.d.).

Figure 11.5 The Federal Trade Commission was created to oversee fair trade practices. (Credit: Clker-Free-Vector-Images/ pixabay/ License: CC0)

The FTC Act is only enforceable by the Federal Trade Commission (FTC), which was created as a result of this Act (Jurist, 2013). The FTC implements the Act's provisions, and the FTC and the U.S. Department of Justice (DOJ) are the federal agencies responsible for prosecuting violators in either civil or criminal proceedings, depending on the act violated. One remedy that the FTC or DOJ can seek is **divestiture**, which forces the company to give up one or more of its operating functions (West, n.d.). Another remedy is **dissolution**, which would terminate the right of a partnership to exist (West, n.d.).

Exemptions

There are limitations on antitrust laws that have been introduced over the years. These include:

- Labor – A labor union can organize and bargain within the bounds of antitrust laws, as long as it does not combine with a nonlabor group.
- Agriculture and Fisheries – Collective co-ops of agricultural groups or fisheries can form, as long as they do not engage in restraint of trade.
- Foreign Trade – Companies can join forces in cooperative activities involving foreign trade exports, as long as trade within the United States is not restrained.
- Cooperative Research and Production – Small businesses can cooperatively work together on research

joint ventures.

In essence, exemptions are allowed, as long as they do not act to restrain trade in the United States (West, n.d.). Once restraint of trade becomes a factor, the practices are no longer exemptions and are subject to antitrust laws.

Conclusion

The three main antitrust laws, namely the Sherman Act, the Clayton Act, and the Federal Trade Commission Act, all work to prevent unfair trade practices that can substantially harm free competition. They also work to protect consumers from practices that would control pricing or the ability to buy or engage in services. They prevent companies from taking actions that would allow them to become too big or too powerful, thus controlling how, and what, consumers and other businesses can do.

Assessment Questions

1. All of the following are forms of restraint of trade that company might use to reduce competition except:

a. Monopolies.
b. Oversupply.
c. Price-fixing.
d. Mergers.

2. What is a Business Trust?

3. Distinguish between naked restraint and ancillary restraint.

4. What was the first antitrust law enacted?.

a. The Clayton Act.
b. The Federal Trade Commission Act.
c. The Antitrust Act.
d. The Sherman Act.

5. What was the original purpose of antitrust legislation?

6. What recourse does the FTC have if an individual or company engages in an unfair trade practice?

a. Consent order.
b. Administrative complaint.
c. Litigation.
d. All of the above.

7. Each state has its own Antitrust law.

a. True.
b. Fasle.

8. Which of the following is not prohibited by the Sherman Act?

a. Temporary limited restraints.
b. Temporary restraints.
c. Naked restraints.
d. Ancillary restraints.

9. Which of the following are possible penalties for violation of the Sherman Act?
   a. Up to $100 million for corporations and individuals.
   b. Up to $100 million for individuals.
   c. Up to $100 millions for corporations.
   d. None of these are correct.

10. Which of the following are considered illegal by the Clayton Act?
   a. Price discrimination.
   b. Exclusive dealing contracts.
   c. Corporate mergers.
   d. All of the above.

11. The following are exempt from antitrust laws:
   a. Small businesses.
   b. Coops.
   c. Labor unions.
   d. Agriculture groups even if they engage in restraint of trade.

12. When was the Federal Trade Commission established?
   a. 1912.
   b. 1914.
   c. 1916.
   d. 1920.

13. The following are bureaus of the Federal Trade Commission except:
   a. Bureau of Unfair Trade Practices.
   b. Bureau of Consumer Protection.
   c. Bureau of Competition.
   d. Bureau Economics.

14. What is the mission of the Bureau of Competition?

15. Explain the Wheeler-Lea Act.

Endnotes

Sources

Federal Trade Commission (n.d.). The antitrust laws. Retrieved from: https://www.ftc.gov/tips-advice/competition-guidance/guide-antitrust-laws/antitrust-laws.

Jurist (2013). History of antitrust laws. Retrieved from: https://www.jurist.org/archives/feature/a-history-and-the-main-acts/.

United States Department of Justice (n.d.). Antitrust laws and you. Retrieved from: https://www.justice.gov/atr/antitrust-laws-and-you.

West's Encyclopedia of American Law (n.d.). Antitrust law. Retrieved from: http://iris.nyit.edu/~shartman/mba0101/trust.htm.

12

Unfair Trade Practices and the Federal Trade Commission

Figure 12.1 (Credit: Carol M. Highsmith collection/ wikimedia/ Attribution 2.0 Generic (CC BY 2.0))

Chapter Outline

12.1 Unfair Trade Practices
12.2 The Federal Trade Commission

Introduction

Learning Outcomes

- Analyze laws pertaining to unfair trade practices and the agency that scrutinizes them.

12.1 Unfair Trade Practices

The term "unfair trade practice" describes the use of deceptive, fraudulent, or unethical methods to gain business advantage or to cause injury to a consumer. Unfair trade practices are considered unlawful under the Consumer Protection Act. The purpose of the law is to ensure that consumers have the opportunity to make informed, rational decisions about the goods and services they purchase.

Unfair trade practices include false representation of a good or service, targeting vulnerable populations, false advertising, tied selling, false free prize or gift offers, false or deceptive pricing, and non-compliance with manufacturing standards. Alternative names for unfair trade practices are "deceptive trade practices" or "unfair business practices."

Section 5(a) (https://www.federalreserve.gov/boarddocs/supmanual/cch/ftca.pdf) of the Federal Trade Commission Act prohibits "unfair or deceptive acts or practices in or affecting commerce." Per the rule, unfair practices are those that cause, or are likely to cause, injury to consumers, those that consumers cannot avoid, and those in which the benefits of the product or service do not outweigh the deception. Deceptive practices are defined as those in which the seller misrepresents or misleads the consumer, and the misleading practice is substantial.

The Federal Trade Commission (FTC) is a federal agency that enforces consumer protection laws. Consumers may seek recourse for unfair trade practices by suing for compensatory or punitive damages. Plaintiffs do not have to prove intent. Showing that the practice itself was unfair or deceptive is sufficient.

Figure 12.2 The Federal Trade Commission (FTC) enforces consumer protection laws. (Credit: U.S. Government/ wikimedia/ License: Public Domain)

Unfair Trade Practices and Examples

Product Guarantees and False Endorsements

Companies must be prepared to honor product guarantees. For example, if a product is advertised with a 50 percent money-back guarantee, then that must be provided to customers who meet the requirement(s) attached to the guarantee. Similarly, companies may not create false endorsements and testimonials about their products.

Unfair Advertising

False advertising includes the misrepresentation of a product, service, or price. It may be more expansively defined to include unfair sales strategies, such as advertising one item and then selling another item in its place, e.g., one that is higher priced, lower quality and/or less in demand. This method is most commonly referred to as "bait and switch." Additional examples of unfair advertising include incorrect pricing, fake endorsements, deceptive guarantees, making false statements, and providing descriptions that exaggerate the performance of the product or service.

EXAMPLE 12.1

For months, Ivan had searched for just the right window curtain to match the décor of his new high rise condo. Finally, while browsing through Amazon, he saw two gray velvet curtains that featured a damask pattern, with taupe and gold accents and specks of ice blue glitter accents. He could not have designed a more perfect color palette for the window treatments if he tried. Moreover, the velvet blackout touch was just what he needed. Excited, he hit the "Buy Now" button and waited a couple of days for his order to arrive. When it did, what a huge disappointment! He could see, if he stared long and hard enough, how someone with a vivid imagination might consider the curtain to be an abstract interpretation of what was advertised. However, most people would see that the product was not at all close to what was advertised. The velvet was closer to linen, the damask pattern was closer to swirls, and the taupe and gold accents with specks of ice blue were closer to silver and purple, with specks of mauve. After running a Google reverse image search of the original product photo, he saw it featured in an interior design magazine. When Ivan looked up the product endorsements and reviews, he saw that all of the reviewers had only posted reviews for that particular seller's products, and that they had posted nothing but glowing reviews for each of the products. It was clear to Ivan that the seller was guilty of false advertising, as well as faking endorsements. Ivan has enough information to submit a consumer complaint to the Federal Trade Commission.

Taking Advantage of Customers

The FTC also pays particular attention to business ventures that target vulnerable populations. For example, some telemarketing efforts employ intense pressuring tactics to target seniors and people who don't speak English.

EXAMPLE 12.2

Devin is involved in the telemarketing of spy gadgets, such as bugs and bug detectors. He has had a lot of trouble finding a market for these products. One day, he speaks with an older citizen who asks him about the benefits of the bug detector. Devin starts to knowingly make unsubstantiated claims that there have been news reports that home bugging is on the rise. His false claims works like a charm. Spooked, the elderly customer buys the most expensive bug detector product. Seeing his success, Devin purchases a report of households in his geographic selling area that are headed by people over the age of 70. Over the next few months, his sales increase at an explosive rate. When he is recognized by management for his leading sales numbers, they also inquire about the secret to his success as they seek to replicate it in training materials for other sales professionals. When Devin proudly explains his tactics, he is terminated by the company. The company calls the customers impacted by his false claims, explains that there was a misrepresentation by one their sales associates regarding the scope of known bugging activity, allows them to keep their bug detectors, and refunds them the money they spent purchasing the products. The sales associate engaged in unfair trade practices, but the company took appropriate steps to correct it.

Misrepresenting a Product

At times, the FTC may be quite technical in its definition of certain terms. For this reason, companies should be very clear about their usage of various phrases and words. For example, the word "new" may only be used to refer to a product that is less than six months old. Other terms may be the subject of debate or litigation, such as whether a lotion will actually "rejuvenate" skin or whether a tablet will actually "cure" baldness. Indeed, a sweater should not be called "wool" unless that is its complete composition. There are many examples, so it is important for businesses to have an understanding of the FTC's rules on this topic.

Giving Misleading Price Information

The FTC sanctions misleading price information as an unfair trade practice. Examples of misleading price information include false sales in which a "limited time offer" might actually be available forever, or running a "Going Out of Business" sale without any plans to go out of business while advertising that items are discounted, although the prices have not changed.

EXAMPLE 12.3

A brick and mortar store has an online promotion for a "buy one, get one" offer for the season's hottest new phone, stating that the offer is only available on Black Friday. The store opens at 5:00 a.m., and customers start lining up with their sleeping bags in tow the evening prior to the morning opening time. After customers almost stampede one another, they learn that they will have to also purchase a phone plan that is inflated by 100% of its regular price to qualify for the deal. Nowhere in the literature or promotions was the phone plan, or its over-inflated price, mentioned as a requirement to get the buy one get one free phone deal.

Failing to Disclose Pertinent Information

Merchants must disclose facts that would reasonably influence the consumer's decision to make a purchase. Withholding pertinent information from customers may be viewed by the FTC as equal in severity to the process of using overtly incorrect or deceptive information. For example, sellers should always disclose the full price of their products or services before accepting payment for them.

12.2 The Federal Trade Commission

The FTC was created in 1914 to address the problem of monopolies and trusts. Following the Civil War, a wave of consolidation and growth among companies triggered increased public debate. Through handshake agreements, issuance of stock, and pooling arrangements, companies could fix prices and outputs, thus effectively stopping competition and raising consumer prices. A substantial number of mergers gave control over key industries to small groups of businesses. Where companies did not merge, other arrangements were made to have a similar effect. Conglomerates controlled most of the relevant industries that produced household necessities. Goods used in production were also the product of highly concentrated trusts, such as the United States Steel Corporation and the International Paper Company. Concerns about industrialization and a changing economy, with shifting norms for personal lives, triggered antitrust sentiment.

Figure 12.3 The Federal Trade Commission prevents monopolies, like that of U.S. Steel in the early 20th century. (Credit: Bruce McAllister/ wikimedia/ License: Public Domain)

The perceived unfairness and fears caused by the consolidation of businesses created strong anti-business sentiment and increasing cries for price controls to be considered as a remedy for heavily concentrated industries. These organizations posed economic and social problems that became a large social concern. In response, the Federal Trade Commission (FTC) was created with broad powers to investigate and propose formal recommendations to companies about their competitive practices. The FTC did not formally have a consumer protection mission until the passage of the Wheeler-Lea Act in 1938. This act gave the FTC the power to combat false advertising for any foods, drugs, medical devices, or cosmetics.

In addition to the Wheeler-Lea Act, subsequent amendments to the FTC Act, as well as judicial respect toward the agency, broadened the power and jurisdiction of the FTC.

Today, in addition to its original antitrust roots, the FTC enforces consumer protection laws.

Bureaus of the FTC

Several bureaus now stand in support of the FTC's efforts.

Bureau of Consumer Protection

The Bureau of Consumer Protection protects consumers against unfair trade practices. Bureau attorneys enforce consumer protection laws issued by the FTC. In addition to enforcement actions, the Bureau's functions include investigations and consumer and business training. Unfair trade practices in advertising and marketing are a main focus, as well as privacy, financial products and practices, and identity protection. The Bureau also manages the United States National Do Not Call Registry and investigates telemarketing fraud.

Bureau of Competition

The Bureau of Competition's purpose is to eliminate and prevent "anticompetitive" business practices related to the enforcement of antitrust laws. The FTC and the Department of Justice share responsibility for enforcement of antitrust laws.

Bureau of Economics

The Bureau of Economics supports the Bureau of Competition and Bureau of Consumer Protection by providing subject matter expertise regarding the economic impacts of FTC legislative activity.

FTC Activities

The FTC investigates issues raised through a number of sources, including consumer, business, and media reports. If the FTC concludes that there was unlawful conduct, it may seek several forms of recourse. These include the pursuit of voluntary compliance through a consent order, the submission and filing of administrative complaints, or the initiation of a federal action and litigation.

The FTC has the power to create rules regarding widespread industry practices. Rules created in this fashion to address systemic issues are called trade rules.

Assessment Questions

1. Define unfair trade practices.

2. All of the following are considered unfair trade practices except:
   a. Targeting vulnerable populations.
   b. Charging extremely high prices.
   c. False advertising.
   d. False representation of a good or service.

3. What is a bait and switch?

4. Describe the role of the Federal Trade Commission.

5. The following are examples of a company giving misleading price information except:
   a. Advertising "Limited Time Offer" when the offer is available forever.
   b. Advertising "Going Out of Business" when the company plans to stay in business.
   c. Advertising the product as "New" when the product is more than 6 months old.
   d. Advertising "Buy One, Get One" without informing consumers that they must buy another product or service to get the deal.

Endnotes

The Consumer Protection Act: Unfair Trade Practices. Retrieved from: https://www.ftc.gov.bb/library/2003-06-13_unfair_trade_practices.pdf.

Lumen Learning. (n.d.). Business and the Legal Environment. Retrieved from:

https://courses.lumenlearning.com/buslegalenv/chapter/27-3-unfair-trade-practices/.

Holt, W. S. (2010). *Federal trade commission: Its history, activities and organization*. Gale Ecco, Making Of Mode.

About the FTC. (2018, July 17). Retrieved from: https://www.ftc.gov/about-ftc.

Consumer Information, Federal Trade Commission. (n.d.). Retrieved from: https://www.consumer.ftc.gov/.

Federal Trade Commission, USA.gov. (n.d.). Retrieved from: https://www.usa.gov/federal-agencies/federal-trade-commission.

Statutes Enforced or Administered by the Commission. (n.d.). Retrieved from: https://www.ftc.gov/enforcement/statutes.

13 International Law

Figure 13.1 (Credit: geralt/ pixabay/ Attribution 2.0 Generic (CC BY 2.0))

Chapter Outline

13.1 Introduction to International Law
13.2 Sources and Practice of International Law

Introduction

Learning Outcome

- Explain international law and its role in business.

13.1 Introduction to International Law

In 1945, President Harry Truman stated, “When Kansas and Colorado have a quarrel over the water in the Arkansas River they don’t call out the National Guard in each state and go to war over it. They bring a suit in the Supreme Court of the United States and abide by the decision. There isn’t a reason in the world why we cannot do that internationally” (Cheeseman, 2016, p. 903). Customs, which vary among global communities and international organizations, are a primary reason why the world cannot pursue such an answer to trade and commerce dealings. The priorities and aims for Chinese businesses differ from those of Brazil. Each of those two countries have radically different business perspectives from the United States. For this reason, international law utilizes customs, treaties, and organizations to guide relationships among nations, with the goal of allowing each country as much leverage as possible over its own business dealings.

Figure 13.2 International laws are based on customs, treaties, and organizations that guide partnerships among nations. (Credit: GDJ/ pixabay/ License: CC0)

International Law

International law relates to the policies and procedures that govern relationships among nations (Clarkson, Miller, & Cross, 2018). These are crucial for businesses for multiple reasons. First, there is not a single authoritative legislative source for global business affairs, nor a single world court responsible for interpreting international law (Cheeseman, 2016, p. 903). There is also not a global executive branch that enforces international law, which leaves global business affairs particularly vulnerable.

Secondly, if a nation violates an international law and persuasive tactics fail, then the countries that were violated, or international organizations tasked with overseeing global trade, may act. Often these actions use force to correct the offenses and may include economic sanctions, severance of diplomatic relations, boycotts, or even war against the offending nation (Clarkson, Miller, & Cross, 2018, p. 439).

The purpose of international laws is to permit countries as much authority as possible over their own international business affairs, while maximizing economic benefits of trade and working relationships with other nations. Since many countries have historically allowed governance by international agreements when conducting global business, there exists an evolving body of international laws that facilitate global trade and commerce.

U.S. Constitutional Clauses

There are two important clauses in the U.S. Constitution related to international law. First, the **Foreign Commerce Clause** enables Congress to "regulate commerce with foreign nations" (Cheeseman, 2016, p. 904). This clause permits U.S. businesses to actively negotiate and implement taxes or other regulations as they relate to international commerce. However, businesses cannot unduly burden foreign commerce. For example, General Motors, which is based in Michigan, cannot suggest that the state impose a 50 percent tax on foreign-made automobiles sold in the state, while not imposing the same tax on U.S.-made vehicles. Michigan can, however, impose a 10 percent tax on all automobile sales in the state to offset the costs of foreign trade and commerce.

The second important clause related to international law is the **Treaty Clause**, which states that the president has the power "by and with the advice and consent of the senate" to create treaties with other nations (Clarkson, Miller, & Cross, 2018, p. 440). This clause restricts treaties to federal authority, meaning that states do not have the power to enter a treaty with another nation. For example, the United States and Mexico can sign a treaty to reduce trade barriers between both nations, but the state of Texas cannot sign a treaty with Mexico to reduce trade barriers between Texas businesses and Mexico. Additionally, any treaties established with other countries become U.S. law, and any conflicting law is null and void.

Primary Sources of International Law

International customs, treaties, and organizations are the primary sources of international law (Clarkson, Miller, & Cross, 2018, p. 439).

Figure 13.3 Three distinct components are sources for how international law is understood, defined, and interpreted around the world. (Modification of art by BNED Credit: CC BY NC SA)

These three components work together to guide how nations understand, define, and interpret international laws that govern global business affairs.

International Customs

Customs are general practices between nations that guide their business relationships. According to the

Statute of the International Court of Justice, international customs are "accepted as law" (Clarkson, Miller, & Cross, 2018, p. 439). While customary international law (CIL) is not written, nor does it require ratification to become binding, CIL nonetheless provides guidelines for how nations conduct business affairs (Bradley & Gulati, 2010, p. 204). One example of a custom is the international protection of ambassadors. For thousands of years, ambassadors have been protected while serving diplomatic missions. For this reason, countries protect foreign ambassadors with the understanding that any harm caused to ambassadors would be a violation of international law.

International Treaties

Treaties and other agreements between nations are authorized and ratified by the countries that acknowledge their legality. There are two different types of agreements: bilateral, which is formed by two nations; and multilateral, which is formed by several nations. The Peru-United States Trade Promotion Agreement is an example of a bilateral agreement. It was signed in 2006, ratified by Peru the same year, and ratified by the United States in 2007. This bilateral agreement is considered beneficial to the United States because it improves access to Peruvian goods, while promoting security and democracy in the South American country. The North American Free Trade Agreement, or NAFTA, is an example of a multilateral agreement. It was ratified in 1994, when Mexico joined the previous trade agreement between the United States and Canada. In September 2018, the Trump administration successfully completed re-negotiations with Mexico and Canada that lasted over one year. Among other aims, these negotiations worked to increase auto industry wages for workers in Mexico and modify pharmaceutical regulations with Canada.

International Organizations

International organizations are comprised of officials who represent member nations that have established a treaty to oversee shared interests, including trade and commerce. The U.S. participates in more than 120 bilateral and multilateral organizations around the world. International organizations adopt resolutions that standardize behavior and create uniform rules related to trade and commerce. Two of the most significant international organizations established in the twentieth century that significantly impact U.S. trade and commerce are the United Nations and the European Union.

United Nations

The **United Nations (UN)** was created as a multilateral treaty in 1945. The UN's organizational goals include maintaining global peace and security, promoting economic and social cooperation, and protecting human rights, especially related to women and children (Cheeseman, 2016, p. 905). The UN **General Assembly** includes representatives from each member nation. As of 2018, the UN acknowledges 195 sovereign states, with all but two participating as full members. These two, Palestine and the Vatican City, are classified as "observer states." Six additional countries are not UN members, but are recognized as a country by at least one UN member country: Abkhazia, Kosovo, Northern Cypress, South Ossetia, Taiwan, and Western Sahara.

The UN **Security Council** includes five permanent members and 10 countries selected by the General Assembly to serve two-year terms. The five countries that hold permanent membership are China, France, Russia, the United Kingdom, and the United States (Cheeseman, 2016, p. 558). This Council is primarily responsible for overseeing global peace and security measures. The World Bank is a UN organization, financed by contributions from developed countries and headquartered in Washington, D.C. Its primary functions include providing money to developing countries to fund projects that relieve suffering, including building roads and dams, establishing hospitals, developing agriculture, and other humanitarian efforts. The World Bank provides both grants and long-term low interest rate loans to countries, often granting debt relief for outstanding loans (Cheeseman, 2016, p. 559).

The United Nations Commission International Trade Law is one of the most important international organizations to date, establishing the 1980 Convention on Contracts for the International Sale of Goods (CISG), which will be discussed further in the next section.

European Union

The **European Union (EU)** is a regional international organization that includes many countries in Europe. It was established to create peace across the region and promote economic, social, and cultural development (Cheeseman, 2016, p. 561). As of 2018, there are 28 countries affiliated with the EU, although the United Kingdom has begun steps to withdraw its membership. Additionally, Macedonia is actively seeking a path toward EU membership, although as of September 2018, the country's citizens remain divided. The EU organization has established a treaty for its members that creates open borders for trade among member nations, especially for capital, labor, goods, and services. The impact on U.S. commerce is significant, as the EU represents more than 500 million people and a gross community product that exceeds that of the United States, Canada, and Mexico combined (Cheeseman, 2016, p. 561).

Sovereignty

National sovereignty defines a nation. While clearly defined borders and independent governments also set parameters for a nation, **sovereignty** is an important legal principle that allows nations to enter negotiated treaties with other countries and honor territorial boundaries. It is among the most important international law principles, thus greatly impacting international trade and commerce.

Since the 1800s, most established nations allowed for absolute sovereignty among the global community. However, by the 1940s, that allowance was significantly reduced, as countries revisited sovereignty in light of globalization, transportation, and communication advances, and the rise of international organizations (Goldsmith, 2000, p. 959). Consequentially, doctrines of limited immunity were created that established guidelines for how countries may prosecute, or hold foreign nationals accountable, during international trade and commerce dealings.

A **doctrine of sovereign immunity** states that countries are granted immunity from lawsuits in courts of other countries (p. 569). Although the United States initially granted absolute immunity to foreign governments from lawsuits in U.S. courts, in 1952, the United States adapted federal law to qualified immunity, which is the immunity regulation adopted in most Western nations. This law led to the **Foreign Sovereign Immunities Act of 1976**, allowing U.S. governance over lawsuits against other nations in the United States in either federal- or state-level courts. Simply stated, a foreign country is not immune to lawsuits in the United States when the country has waived its immunity, or if the commercial activity against which the lawsuit is intended causes a direct effect in the United States.

13.2 Sources and Practice of International Law

International law is primarily governed by customs, treaties, and organizations that influence how laws are understood, interpreted, and enforced around the world. Since there is not a central court to enforce international law, each country utilizes its own courts to settle disputes. Collective action, reciprocity, and shaming are three examples of non-legislative methods that influence trade when enacted against nations that violate international law.

Figure 13.4 International laws are enforced through positive and punitive measures that seek to uphold the global integrity of trade and commerce among all nations. (Credit: qimono/ pixabay/ CC0)

Sources of International Law

The sources of international law are customs, treaties, and organizations, as discussed in the previous section. These three components work synergistically to influence how the international community facilitates business trade and commerce. More importantly, international law is enforced when a country violates the principles set forth by globally shared customs, treaties, and organizations.

One of the most important governing documents for international law is the **United Nations Convention on Contracts for the International Sale of Goods (CISG)**, which was established in 1980. This law governs contracts of countries that have ratified it as the priority contract for trade. By January 2018, 84 countries had adopted CISG, including the countries that account for more than two-thirds of all global trade. Those countries include the United States, Canada, China, Japan, Mexico, Argentina, Brazil, and most European countries. The CISG is enforced whenever international transactions occur without the presence of written contracts to govern those transactions. There are limits to the CISG, however, as the CISG does not apply to consumer sales or contracts for services (Clarkson, Miller, & Cross, 2018, p. 376).

International Principles and Doctrines

There are three significant principles that help establish and enforce international law: the Principle of Comity, the Act of State Doctrine, and the Doctrine of Sovereign Immunity.

The **Principle of Comity** states that nations will defer to the laws and decrees of other nations when those laws are consistent with their own, essentially upholding reciprocity between nations with similar laws. For example, a U.S. court will most likely uphold a business contract as valid even if it was drafted in England, since the United Kingdom's legal procedures are consistent with U.S. procedures (Cross & Miller, 2018, p. 216).

The **Act of State Doctrine** is a law applicable in England and the United States. It states that these two nations will not pass legal judgement on public acts committed by a recognized government if those acts occur within that government's own territory (Cross & Miller, 2018, p. 216). For example, the United States will not file a lawsuit against Petrobras, a Brazilian oil company, alleging price fixing, since the act of pricing oil occurs in Brazil, which is a nation that holds control over its own natural resources.

The **Doctrine of Sovereign Immunity**, which was introduced in the previous section, states that foreign nations are immune from U.S. jurisdiction when certain circumstances are applied. However, there are exceptions to this law. If a foreign country conducts commercial business activity in the United States and an entity in the United States files a lawsuit against the foreign business, then the foreign state is not immune from U.S. jurisdiction (Cross & Miller, 2018, p. 216).

International Law Enforcement

One of the most important considerations for international business is understanding that companies operating in foreign nations are subject to the laws of those nations (Cross & Miller, 2018, p. 212). When international laws are violated, disputes are often resolved through the legal systems within individual nations. Most countries have either common law or civil law systems. **Common law systems** operate independently by developing their own rules that govern areas of business law, such as torts and contracts. The United States has a common law system. One-third of all people in the world live in nations in which common law is practiced. **Civil law systems** base their legislation on Roman civil law, which utilizes statutory codes as the primary source of law (p. 212).

Common Law		**Civil Law**	
Australia	Malaysia	Argentina	Indonesia
Bangladesh	New Zealand	Austria	Iran
Canada	Nigeria	Brazil	Italy
Ghana	Singapore	Chile	Japan
India	United Kingdom	China	Mexico
Israel	United States	Egypt	Poland
Jamaica	Zambia	Finland	South Korea
Kenya		France	Sweden
		Germany	Tunisia
		Greece	Venezuela

Table 13.1

Impact on International Trade

There are three international law enforcement methods that can radically impact trade: collective action, reciprocity, and shaming.

Collective action occurs when businesses work collectively to strengthen their resources and achieve a shared goal. In February 2018, the UN Conference on Trade and Development Secretary-General argued that collective action can be one of the most effective methods for protecting international trade in the current global climate. Due to recent trade restructuring from the United States and the United Kingdom (pending its withdrawal from the EU), collective action was promoted as a way to "harness energy that will not fragment the [international trade] system" (UNCTAD, 2018). By leveraging nations to defend "rules-based multilateral trading systems as a force for creating inclusive prosperity," the Secretary-General promoted collective action as the primary way to assure continued international peace and economic viability for generations to come.

Reciprocity is central to international trade and at the core of CIL. It happens most commonly in international business exchanges as countries lower import duties, or other trade barriers, in exchange for mutual arrangements extended by the other country. Reciprocity can be beneficial to the nations involved, or it can be punitive. In 2016, presidential candidate Donald Trump campaigned for an international trade climate that would produce fairer options for the United States. Since his inauguration, he has increasingly pressured the global community by imposing taxes on imports from Canada, China, the EU, and Mexico, each of which has retaliated in reciprocity. In 2018, China accused the United States of launching the "largest trade war in economic history," of which the final global impacts remain largely unknown (BBC, 2018).

Shaming is a deliberate attempt to negatively impact a state, regime, or governmental leader's reputation by publicizing and targeting violations of international laws, including customary norms, treaty breaches, and violations of organizational expectations (Gopalan & Fuller, 2014, p. 75). However, shaming is not viewed as particularly effective without more concrete measures to accompany it (Klymak, 2017). A recent research study conducted by the Department of Economics in Dublin, Ireland, found that there is no evidence to suggest that there has been a decrease in the imports of goods to the United States from countries where foreign goods are likely produced by child and forced labor. Despite media coverage and the International Labour Organization's coverage that routinely shames certain nations for producing goods by child or forced labor, those goods are nonetheless regularly imported for international sale.

Assessment Questions

1. What is International law?

2. The following are clauses in the U.S. Constitution that relate to international law.

a. Treaty Clause.
b. Foreign Commerce Clause.
c. Both a and b.
d. Neither a nor b.

3. Explain the European Union.

4. What is the Doctrine of Sovereign Immunity?

5. The UN Security Council is made up of:

a. 5 members and 10 countries.
b. 10 members and 5 countries.
c. 10 members and 10 countries.
d. 5 members and 5 countries.

6. Sources of international law include:

a. Customs, treaties, and laws.
b. Customs, treaties, and edict.
c. Treaties, laws, and edicts.
d. Customs, treaties, and organizations.

7. Explain the principle of comity.

8. Compare and contrast common law systems vs. civil law systems.

9. How many countries have adopted the United Nations Convention on Contracts for the International Sale of Goods (CISG)?

a. 74.
b. 84.
c. 94.
d. 104.

10. All of the following are international law enforcement methods except:

a. Collective action.
b. Reciprocity.
c. Shaming.
d. All of the above.

Endnotes

Bradley, C. A., & Gulati, M. (2010). Withdrawing from international custom. *The Yale Law Journal, 120*, 202–275.

Cheeseman, H. (2016). *Business law: Legal environment, online commerce, business ethics, and international issues* (9th ed.). Boston, MA: Pearson Education.

Cheeseman, H. (2016). *Legal environment of business: Online commerce, business ethics, and global issues* (8th ed.). Boston, MA: Pearson Education.

Clarkson, K. W., Miller, R. L., & Cross, F. B. (2018). *Business law: Texts and cases* (14th ed.). Boston, MA: Cengage Learning.

Goldsmith, J. (2000). Review: Sovereignty, international relations theory, and international law. *Stanford Law Review, 52*(4), 959–986.

BBC. (2018, September 18). US-China trade row: What has happened so far? BBC News. Retrieved from: https://www.bbc.com/news/business-44529600.

Clarkson, K. W., Miller, R. L., & Cross, F. B. (2018). Business law: Texts and cases (14th ed.). Boston, MA: Cengage Learning.

Cross, F. B., & Miller, R. L. (2018). The legal environment of business: Texts and cases (10th ed.). Boston, MA: Cengage Learning.

Gopalan, S., & Fuller, R. (2014). Enforcing international law: States, IOs, and courts as shaming reference groups. Brooklyn Journal of International Law, 39(1), 73–158.

Klymak, M. (2017). The trade impacts of naming and shaming of forced and child labor. Trinity Economic Papers, 1–41. Retrieved from: http://www.tcd.ie/Economics/TEP/2017/tep1517.pdf.

UN. (2018, February 19). Collective action is key to defending trade, Geneva dialogue hears. UN Conference on Trade and Development News. Retrieved from: https://unctad.org/en/pages/newsdetails.aspx?OriginalVersionID=1669.

14 Securities Regulation

Figure 14.1 (Credit: Sam Valadi/ flickr/ Attribution 2.0 Generic (CC BY 2.0))

Chapter Outline

14.1 Liability Under the Securities Act
14.2 The Framework of Securities Regulation

Introduction

Learning Outcome

- Describe the Securities Exchange Act of 1934 and its impact on business.

14.1 Liability Under the Securities Act

As explained in the previous section, many companies were initially irritated by the creation of the Securities Exchange Act of 1934, as it created a myriad of legal responsibilities and potential liabilities that impacted their business models. Companies came to recognize that they needed legal counsel and internal systems in place to ensure that they were in compliance. The liabilities for not complying with the Securities and Exchange Act of 1934 include not only monetary fines, but also **civil** penalties, and in some cases, **criminal** proceedings. Insider trading is one violation that can result in criminal charges.

Insider Trading

While laws vary from country to country, **insider trading** can be understood by what the SEC defines as the "buying or selling a security, in breach of a fiduciary duty or other relationship of trust and confidence, on the basis of material, nonpublic information about the security." The word **fiduciary** comes from the Latin word for trust and refers to someone who is charged with the responsibility to act in the best interest of the other party. In the case of businesses, fiduciaries are expected to act in the best interests of their investors. However, they are often aware of information that the public is not. This knowledge has important implications as addressed by Section 10(b) and Rule 10b-5 of the Securities Exchange Act of 1934, which prohibits the purchase or sale of securities on the basis of "**material nonpublic information**,"; meaning information of any kind that would impact the market price of securities that has not been disclosed to the public, i.e., insider information. The directors, large shareholders, and officers of companies frequently have access to nonpublic information that could affect the future value of a security. While an individual, as opposed to an entire company, is often charged as an insider trader, such charges can affect the entire company's reputation, putting it in a negative light and eroding investor trust.

One instance of insider trading that received widespread media attention involved Martha Stewart, who in 2003 became the subject of legal scrutiny after selling her shares in the pharmaceutical company ImClone. Following the advice of her broker, David Bacanovic, Stewart sold all of her shares of ImClone before it lost 16 percent of its value. Bacanovic represented ImClone CEO Sam Waksal, who was selling $5 million of his ImClone shares. While Bacanovic claimed he did not know why, he shared this information with Stewart. As it turned out, the FDA had not approved ImClone's primary pharmaceutical product, Erbitux, which was a setback that only insiders were privy to. Stewart avoided a $45,673 loss by selling her shares before the public announcement. Even though Stewart may not have known exactly why ImClone would go down in value, the court decided that her decision to act upon her broker's suggestion constituted a wrongdoing. Stewart's role as a public figure was also relevant to this decision, as explained by SEC's Director of Enforcement Stephen M. Cutler, who said, "It is fundamentally unfair for someone to have an edge on the market just because she has a stockbroker who is willing to break the rules and give her an illegal tip. It's worse still when the individual engaging in the insider trading is the Chairman and CEO of a public company."

Figure 14.2 Insider trading can result in criminal conviction and possibly jail time. (Credit: Suzy Hazelwood/ pexels/ License: CC0)

Insider trading is not always illegal. In certain instances, individuals in possession of insider knowledge can disclose their trading activity to the SEC. However, disclosure alone is not enough to make trading on the basis of insider information legally acceptable. Another instance in which the officers of publicly held companies can legally transact securities involves **pre-arranged trading plans**. For example, SEC Rule 10b5-1 permits executives at public companies to transact securities so long as it is arranged in good faith beforehand to take place on certain predetermined future dates and involves pre-set amounts. So long as these criteria are followed, they are granted safe harbor. **Safe harbor**, in this context, refers to exemption from insider trading charges for compliant pre-arranged equity trades.

Schedule 13D

In 1968, the Williams Act amended the Securities Exchange Act of 1934 so that investors could have advance warning of possible corporate takeovers. If someone (individual/corporation) becomes the **beneficial owner** of more than 5% of a company's stock, that entity must file a Schedule 13D with the SEC within 10 days of purchase. A beneficial owner is anyone with "voting and investment power over their shares." There are a few exceptions that apply, such as qualified **institutional investors**—large investors who are deemed to have sophisticated knowledge of securities such that they do not need the same level of protection as general investors. Insurance companies, state employee benefits plans, and investment companies are examples of qualified institutional investors who are allowed to report their holdings at the end of the calendar year.

Insider Transactions

Corporate insiders are those officers, directors, and beneficial owners who own more than 10% of a class of securities, registered under Section 12 of the Securities Exchange Act of 1934. Corporate insiders must file a statement of ownership with the SEC to be in compliance, and as of August 27, 2002, the SEC implemented new rules that shortened the time period to report insider transactions. It is important for a company to have internal controls and a system to ensure their corporate insiders are reporting their trades in a timely fashion. Companies that do not implement and enforce compliance procedures can become liable for the actions of their employees who fail to follow the law.

Reporting Requirements

Publicly owned companies that meet certain size requirements are called **reporting companies**, and per Section 13(a) of the Securities Exchange Act of 1934, they must file periodic disclosures. The purpose of these disclosures is to help investors make educated decisions regarding how to invest their money. These reports include information about a company's line of business, corporate officers and directors, and financial statements.

- **Form 10-K**. Form 10-K, also known as the annual report, contains **audited** financial statements. Audited financial statements have been reviewed by one or more CPAs who are not affiliated with the company and who provide an objective opinion about whether or not the financial statements, such as the balance sheet, income statement, statement of changes to retained earnings, and cash flow statement, conform with accounting standards known as the Generally Accepted Accounting Principles (GAAP). When the Securities Exchange Act of 1934 was first passed, most companies' annual reports contained only the bare minimum amount of information. However, over time, companies came to view their annual reports as a way to not only comply with SEC requirements, but also to attract new investors and impress securities analysts, or financial professionals who study various industries to make recommendations on whether a security should be bought, held, or sold. Today, many annual reports contain not only the required facts, but also compelling narratives that detail the company's mission and strategic goals. The annual reports of certain companies—for example, Berkshire Hathaway, written by Warren Buffett and Charlie Munger—provide not only their opinions on their own operations, known as the **management discussion**, but also their thoughts on the economy overall. The Form 10-K is a large responsibility for a company because it must disclose the company's analysis of its financial conditions, potential market risks, internal controls, legal proceedings, defaults, and other information that is deemed important for investors to make sound investment decisions.

- **Form 10-Q**. Form 10-Qs are quarterly **unaudited** financial statements that contain financial information. Since they are unaudited, they are less expensive and time-consuming for the company to prepare; however, investors do not have the additional assurance that they have been analyzed by a neutral CPA.
- **Form 8-K**. Certain events require the company to file a **Form 8-K**, such as a change in the company's officers, mergers, or declarations of bankruptcy. These are required to be filed within four business days with the SEC.
- **Proxy Statements**. Proxy statements are documents that the SEC requires that shareholders of companies with securities registered under Section 12 of the Securities Exchange Act of 1934 receive to allow them to vote on issues that will be decided at a stockholder meeting. This process is commonly applied when voting for directors or deciding corporate actions. Even shareholders who own just one share of a company receive proxy statements; thus, the process of sending out these statements is a large undertaking for companies. While some companies still use the mail to deliver proxy statements, others send a "Notice of Internet Availability of Proxy Materials" to shareholders a minimum of 40 days before the shareholders' meeting.

Ongoing Responsibilities

Businesses must stay current with changes in securities laws that impact their liabilities and responsibilities. The Exchange Act allows the SEC to make new laws, like it did in 2000 with Regulation FD, which stands for "fair disclosure". In 2013, the SEC started to allow the use of social media channels, in certain circumstances, as a means of distributing information to shareholders.

Summary

These two sections have provided an overview of some of the most important points of the Securities Exchange Act of 1934. Considering the sheer number of exceptions and complexities, coupled with today's rapidly changing technological and political climates, a successful company needs competent legal counsel to help it navigate the compliance requirements of the SEC. While certain illegal actions can be due to malicious intent, such as insider trading, this situation is not always the case; a corporate insider can fail to comply simply because he or she is not aware of the nuances of the law.

14.2 The Framework of Securities Regulation

The Securities Exchange Act of 1934

In 1929, the United States stock market crashed and lost $25 billion, which would be approximately $319 billion today. The Stock Market crash of 1929 was one cause of the American Great Depression of the 1930s, which caused the failure of nearly half of American banks and created unemployment rates of almost 25 percent by

This OpenStax book is available for free at http://cnx.org/content/col30149/1.5

1933. These dire economic conditions created the need for **breadlines**, quite literally, hungry people who waited in line at charitable and government organizations for loaves of bread, and **shanty towns**, or areas where families who had lost their homes lived in cloistered tents on the outskirts of cities. Farmers could not even afford to harvest their crops.

Figure 14.3 Florence Owens Thompson and her children were living on frozen vegetables and birds they killed in this famous photograph taken in 1936 in California. (Credit: Dorothea Lange/ wikimedia/ License: Public Domain)

It was amid this social and economic unrest that Congress passed the Securities Exchange Act of 1934. Signed by President Franklin D. Roosevelt, the Securities Exchange Act of 1934 recognized that the stock market crash of 1929 was caused by wild speculation, large and sudden fluctuations, and manipulations involving securities. An article in the 1934 **California Law Review** described the condition of the market at the time by writing,

"Artificial prices of securities were the rule rather than the exception.... The result was vast economic power, with all that implies in a democracy, in the hand of men whose ethical standards were substantially those of gangsters."

Roosevelt wanted to enact legislature to try to prevent this wild speculation in securities from happening again and to restore the public's faith. He recognized that stock market crashes would not only destroy wealth in securities markets, but they were also instrumental to the financial security of the nation as a whole. The passing of the Security Exchange Act of 1934 was not only a reaction to the market crash, but it also represented a broad shift in the social and economic paradigms and legal frameworks of the United States. Previously, the United States had largely followed a **laissez-faire** economic policy. Laissez faire, as popularized by Scottish economist Adam Smith and British philosopher Herbert Spencer, describes an economic philosophy that markets function best when left to their own devices, i.e., without, or with minimal, government involvement or regulations. The rejection of laissez faire was part of a larger social shift that opposed the long hours, unsafe working conditions, and child labor that had become commonplace as a result of the Industrial Revolution.

The SEC

Section 4 of the Securities Exchange Act of 1934 created the **Securities and Exchange Commission (SEC)** to enforce its ongoing mission. The SEC is an independent agency of the United States federal government. It regulates securities laws and regulations. The first chairperson of the SEC was Joseph P. Kennedy, the father of President John F. Kennedy. The SEC is led by five presidentially appointed commissioners and has five divisions: Division of Corporation Finance, Division of Investment Management, Division of Trading and Markets, Division of Enforcement, and Division of Economic and Risk Analysis.

The SEC also oversees **self-regulatory organizations (SROs)**, or private organizations that create and enforce industry standards. These organizations are allowed to "police" themselves, but are subject to compliance with SEC regulations. The various well-known securities exchanges such as the New York Stock Exchange (NYSE), the National Association of Securities Dealers Automated Quotation System (NASDAQ), and the Chicago Board of Options are SROs. Per Section 12(g), companies with total assets exceeding $10 million and with 500 or more owners of any class of securities must register with the SEC unless they meets exemption requirements.

The SEC makes new laws in response to emerging technologies. For example, Title III of the Jumpstart Our Business Startups (JOBS) Act of 2012 was added, and in it, Section 4(a)(6) allows **crowdfunding**, or raising small amounts of money from many people to fund a venture or project, usually over the internet. Crowdfunding transactions are exempt from registration as long as the amount raised does not exceed $1,070,000 in a 12-month period.

Secondary Markets

The Securities Exchange Act of 1934 governs **secondary markets**, or what is typically referred to as the "stock market." In contrast to the **primary market**, which involves the **initial** sale of a security, such as through an **initial public offering (IPO)**, secondary markets involve subsequent buyers and sellers of securities. One key difference is that primary market prices are set in advance, while secondary market prices are subject to constantly changing market valuations, as determined by supply and demand and investor expectations. For example, when Facebook initiated its IPO in May of 2012, the price was $38 per share, and technical issues on the NASDAQ complicated the offering. After the IPO, the stock traded **sideways**, meaning that it stayed within a range that did not indicate strong upward or downward movement. However, Facebook has gone on to trade at values more than four times its initial IPO valuation, due to investor beliefs and expectations. Not all stocks go up in value after their IPO; some vacillate between highs and lows and frustrate investors with their unstable valuation swings.

Figure 14.4 Stocks on the secondary market fluctuate in value. (Credit: 3844328/ pixabay/ License: CC0)

Reporting Requirements

The Securities Exchange Act of 1934 created numerous reporting requirements for public companies. The purpose of these requirements was **transparency**, that is, keeping the public up to date and informed of changes that might impact securities prices. Public companies with securities registered under Section 12 or that are subject to Section 15(d) must file reports with the SEC. Section 12 requires the registration of certain securities and outlines the procedures necessary to do so. Information required by Section 12 includes the nature of the business, its financial structure, the different classes of securities, the names of officers and directors along with their salaries and bonus arrangements, and financial statements. Section 15 requires brokers and dealers to register with the SEC. Individuals who buy and sell securities are considered traders, and therefore, are not subject to filing under Section 15. Section 15(d) requires registered companies to file periodic reports, such as the the annual Form 10-K and the quarterly Form 10-Q. These reports will be explained in detail in the next section of this chapter. The SEC Commission makes these reports available to all investors through the EDGAR website to help them make informed investment decisions.

Registration Requirements

The Securities Act of 1933 required companies initiating securities offers and exchanges to register with the SEC, unless they met exemption criteria. Section 5 of the Securities Exchange Act of 1934 built upon this foundation and made it unlawful to transact on unregistered exchanges and specifically extended this regulation to the usage of the mail and interstate commerce. 15 U.S. Code § 78f states that exchanges must not only register with the SEC, but they must also have rules that "prevent fraudulent and manipulative acts and practices, to promote just and equitable principles of trade, to foster cooperation and coordination with persons engaged in regulating, clearing, settling, processing information with respect to, and facilitating transactions in securities, to remove impediments to and perfect the mechanism of a free and open market and a national market system, and, in general, to protect investors and the public interest ..."

Blue Sky Laws

When the Securities Exchange Act is discussed, **blue sky laws** are often mentioned. In 1911, Kansas bank commissioner J.N. Dolley became concerned about what he called "swindles," in which investors at the time lost money by investing in "fake mines" or "a Central American plantation that was nine parts imagination." Therefore, he lobbied for the first "comprehensive" securities law in the United States because, as he phrased it, these investments were backed by nothing except the blue skies of Kansas. So, state-level securities laws aimed to combat fraud are called blue sky laws. The SEC does not have jurisdiction over activities within states and does not enforce blue sky laws.

Figure 14.5 In addition to the Securities Exchange Act of 1934, blue sky laws provide an additional state-level layer of legal protection for the public. (Credit: Elia Clerici/ pexels/ License: CC0)

Assessment Questions

1. Explain a laissez-faire economic policy.

2. The following are examples of self-regulatory organizations that the SEC oversees:

a. The New York Stock Exchange.
b. The National Association of Securities Dealers.
c. The Chicago Board of Options.
d. All of the above.

3. Which types of companies must register with the SEC?

a. Companies with over 500 or more owners.
b. Companies with total assets of $10 million.
c. Companies with total assets exceeding $10 million and with 500 or more owners.
d. None of the above.

4. Explain Blue Sky laws.

5. Distinguish between primary markets and secondary markets.

6. Define insider trading.

7. All of the following are considered reports required by the Securities Exchange Act of 1934 except:

a. Form 8k.
b. Form 10 k.
c. Form 10Q.
d. All of the above.

8. Corporate insiders include officers, directors, and beneficial owners who own ____ % of a class of securities registered under Section 12 of the Securities Exchange Act of 1934.

a. 5.
b. 10.
c. 15.
d. 20.

9. Explain Schedule 13D.

10. What's the purpose of Proxy Statements?

Endnotes

Fischel, D. R. (1981). Secondary Liability under Section 10 (b) of the Securities Act of 1934. *California Law Review*, *69*(1), 80–111.

Hanna, J. (1934). The Securities Exchange Act of 1934. *California Law Review*, 1–29.

Horwitz, B., & Kolodny, R. (1977). Line of business reporting and security prices: An analysis of an SEC disclosure rule. *The Bell Journal of Economics*, 234–249.

Jaffe, J. F. (1974). Special information and insider trading. *The Journal of Business*, *47*(3), 410–428.

SEC charges Martha Stewart, Peter Bacanovic with illegal insider trading. U.S. Securities and Exchange Commission. Retrieved from: https://www.sec.gov/news/press/2003-69.htm.

Myers, M. (1994). Rhetoric Hewn by Audience and History: The Evolution of the Annual Report as a Business Document. Retrieved from: https://files.eric.ed.gov/fulltext/ED370138.pdf.

What's the deal with Regulation M. Latham & Watkins Capital Markets Group. Retrieved from: https://www.lw.com/thoughtLeadership/regulation-m-guide-faq.

Engle, E. (2006). What you don't know can hurt you: human rights, shareholder activism and SEC reporting requirements. *Syracuse Law. Review*, *57*, 63.

If you had invested right after facebook's IPO (FB, TWTR). Investopedia. Retrieved from:

https://www.investopedia.com/articles/markets/081415/if-your-would-have-invested-right-after-facebooks-ipo.asp.

Macey, J. R., & Miller, G. P. (1991). Origin of the blue sky laws. *Texas. Law Review*, *70*, 347.

Payne, W. (1911) How Kansas drove out a set of thieves. *The Saturday Evening Post, 184*, 23.

Regulation Crowdfunding: A Small Entity Compliance Guide for Issuers. (n.d). U.S. Securities and Exchange Commission. Retrieved from: https://www.sec.gov/info/smallbus/secg/rccomplianceguide-051316.htm#_ftn1.

Soifer, A. (1987). The Paradox of Paternalism and Laissez-Faire Constitutionalism: United States Supreme Court, 1888–1921. *Law and History Review*, *5*(1), 249–279.

Suddath, C. (October, 2008). The crash of 1929. *Time*. Retrieved from: http://content.time.com/time/nation/article/0,8599,1854569,00.html.

What we do. (n.d). U.S. Securities and Exchange Commission. Retrieved from: https://www.sec.gov/Article/whatwedo.html.

White, E. N. (1990). The stock market boom and crash of 1929 revisited. *Journal of Economic perspectives*, *4*(2), 67–83.

Answer Key

Chapter 1

1. b
3. a
5. a
7. d
9. *What is the supreme law of the land?* The federal constitution is the supreme law of the land. *What are statutes?* Laws enacted by Congress or a state legislative body. *What are ordinances?* Laws enacted by local legislative bodies. *What are administrative rules?* Laws issued by administrative agencies under the authority given to them in statutes.
11. The term "unfair trade practices" is broadly used and refers to any deceptive or fraudulent business practice or act that causes injury to a consumer. Some examples include, but are not limited to, false representations of a good or service including deceptive pricing, non-compliance with manufacturing standards, and false advertising. The FTC investigates allegations of unfair trade practices raised by consumers and businesses, pre-merger notification filings, congressional inquiries, or reports in the media and may seek voluntary compliance by offending businesses through a consent order, administrative complaints, or federal litigation.
13. c
15. b

Chapter 2

1. a
3. The process by which parties with nonidentical preferences allocate resources through interpersonal activity and joint decision making.
5.

The Thomas-Kilmann Conflict Mode Instrument (TKI) is a questionnaire that provides a systematic framework for categorizing five broad negotiation styles. It is closely associated with work done by conflict resolution experts Dean Pruitt and Jeffrey Rubin. These styles are often considered in terms of the level of self-interest, instead of how other negotiators feel. These five general negotiation styles include:

Forcing. If a party has high concern for itself, and low concern for the other party, it may adopt a competitive approach that only takes into account the outcomes it desires. This negotiation style is most prone to zero-sum thinking. For example, a car dealership that tries to give each customer as little as possible for his or her trade-in vehicle would be applying a forcing negotiation approach. While the party using the forcing approach is only considering its own selfinterests, this negotiating style often undermines the party's long-term success. For example, in the car dealership example, if a customer feels she has not received a fair trade-in value after the sale, she may leave negative reviews and will not refer her friends and family to that dealership and will not return to it when the time comes to buy another car. Collaborating.

Collaborating. If a party has high concern and care for both itself and the other party, it will often employ a collaborative negotiation that seeks to maximum the gain for both. In this negotiating style, parties recognize that acting in their mutual interests may create greater value and synergies.

Compromising. A compromising approach to negotiation will take place when parties share some concerns for both themselves and the other party. While it is not always possible to collaborate, parties can often find certain points that are more important to one versus the other, and in that way, find ways to isolate what is most important to each party.

7. a
9.

E-mediation can be useful in situations where the parties are geographically far apart, or the transaction in dispute took place online. Ebay uses e-mediation to handle the sheer volume of misunderstandings between parties. Research has shown that one of the benefits of e-mediation is that it allows people the time needed to "cool down" when they have to explain their feelings in an email, as opposed to speaking to others in person.

In addition to technological advancements, new findings in psychology are influencing how disputes are resolved, such as the rising interest in canine-assisted mediation (CAM), in which the presence of dogs is posited to have an impact on human emotional health. Since the presence of dogs has a positive impact on many of the neurophysiological stress markers in humans, researchers are beginning to explore the use of therapy animals to assist in dispute resolution.

11. c
13. In binding arbitration, the decision of the arbitrator is final, and except in rare circumstances, neither party can appeal the decision through the court system. In non-binding arbitration, the arbitrator's award can be thought of as a recommendation: it is only finalized if both parties agree that it is an acceptable solution.
15. c

Chapter 3

1. Acceptable levels of behavior for each individual who makes up the organization.
3. b
5. a
7. The earliest published book about the topic is *Corporate Responsibility of the Businessman*, published in 1953. This book introduced the concept of companies giving back as a form of investment in the future. This idea came from a generation that had survived some of the hardest times in our world and wanted to make it a better place for generations to come.
9. d

Chapter 4

1.

The authority of the federal government to regulate interstate commerce has, at times, come into conflict with state authority over the same area of regulation. The courts have tried to resolve these conflicts with reference to the police power of the states.

Police power refers to the residual powers granted to each state to safeguard the welfare of their inhabitants. Examples of areas in which states tend to exercise their police power are zoning regulations, building codes, and sanitation standards for eating places. However, there are times when the states' use of police power impacts interstate commerce. If the exercise of the power interferes with, or discriminates against, interstate commerce, then the action is generally deemed to be unconstitutional. The limitation on the authority of states to regulate in areas that impact interstate commerce is known as the dormant commerce clause.

In using the dormant commerce clause to resolve conflicts between state and federal authority, the courts consider the extent to which the state law has a legitimate purpose. If it is determined that the state law has a legitimate purpose, then the court tries to determine whether the impact on interstate commerce is in the interest of the citizens of the state, and will rule accordingly. For instance, an ordinance that banned spray paint, issued in the city of Chicago, was challenged by paint manufacturers under the dormant commerce clause, but was ultimately upheld by the U.S. Court of Appeals because the ban was intended to reduce graffiti and related crimes.

3. d
5. c
7. c
9. a

Chapter 5

1. White collar crimes are characterized by deceit, concealment, or violation of trust. They are committed by business professionals. They generally involve fraud, and the employees committing the crimes are motivated by the desire for financial gains or fear of losing business standing, money, or property. Fraud is the

intentional misrepresentation of material facts for monetary gain. This type of crime is not dependent on threats or violence.
3. d
5. The Foreign Corrupt Practices Act prohibits bribery payments by U.S. companies to foreign government officials with an intent to influence foreign business results. One example of bribery would be a situation in which a pharmaceutical company offers special benefits to individuals who agree to prescribe their medications.
7. b
9. d

Chapter 6

1. Torts are wrongs committed against others who suffer some form of damage as a result.
3. d
5. a
7. b
9. a

Chapter 7

1. A contract is defined as an agreement between two or more parties that is enforceable by law.
3. d
5. b
7. d
9. If a person lacks the mental capacity to enter a contract, then either he or she, or his or her legal guardian, may void it, except in cases where the contract involved necessities. In most states, mental capacity is measured against the "cognitive standard" of whether the party understood its meaning and effect.
11. A material breach is when something substantially different from what was expected under the terms of the contract is delivered, the breach is considered material.
13. Rescission terminates the duties of both parties under the contract, while reformation allows courts to equitably change the contracts substance.
15. Restitution restores the injured party to status quo or the position they had prior to the formation of the contract, by returning the plaintiff any money or property give pursuant to the contract.

Chapter 8

1. A sales contract is s specific type of contract is which one party is obligated to deliver to deliver and transfer ownership of a good to a second party, who in turn is obligated to pay for the good in money, or its equivalent.
3. b
5. A shipment contract occurs when it is the responsibility of the seller to make the shipping arrangements and to transfer the goods to the common carrier. Under this contract, title passes to the buyer at the time of shipment, so the buyer bears the risk of loss, even when he or she has not taken possession of the goods. A destination contract occurs when the seller is required to deliver the goods to a location that is stipulated in the contract. Under this contract, title transfers when the goods are delivered, but the seller bears the risk of loss until that time.
7. An express warranty is one in which the seller explicitly guarantees the quality of the good or service sold. Typically, the vendor provides a statement, or other binding document, as part of the sales contract. In certain circumstances where no express warranty was made, the law implies a warranty. This statement means that the warranty automatically arises from the fact that a sale was made.
9. d

Chapter 9

1. Compared to other countries in the West, stringent and extensive employee protections came fairly late to the United States. Up until 1959, for example, employers had the right to fire a worker without giving any reason. This concept, which was known as at-will employment, was applicable in all states. The concept of at-will employment does, however, continue today, and all employees are considered to be at-will unless they are employed under a collective bargaining agreement, or under a contract for a set duration. Employers can still fire employees for any reason, but they cannot be fired for illegal reasons, as set out in the U.S. or state constitutions, federal law, state statutes, or public policy. In this section, some of the main employee rights and company responsibilities will be introduced.
3. a
5. d

7. A trade union, or labor union, is an organized group of workers who come together to lobby employers about conditions affecting their work.
9. b
11. The Civil Rights Act provides broad provisions pertaining to citizens' civil rights. Title VII of the Civil Rights Act deals with discrimination in employment. It bans employers from discriminating against employees in their hiring, firing, and promotion practices on the basis of sex, national origin, color, religion, or race. All employers who are engaged in commercial activity and who employ 15 or more employees for 20 consecutive weeks in a year are covered by the Act.
13. c
15. a

Chapter 10

1. Administrative law is also referred to as regulatory and public law. It is the law that is related to administrative agencies. Administrative agencies are established by statutes and governed by rules, regulations and orders, court decisions, judicial orders, and decisions.
3. c
5. The FDA was created to protect the public's health. The agency's responsibilities are very broad. The agency fulfills its role by ensuring the safety and effectiveness of drugs consumed by people and animals, biological products, medical devices, food, and cosmetics.
7. d
9. c

Chapter 11

1. b
3. Naked restraint occurs as contracts promote a general restraint of competition. If the restraint was created with a goal of long-term impact without boundaries, it was considered to be a naked restraint. Ancillary restraint occurs as the restriction is limited in time and geography. With ancillary restraint, the restraint would be short-term and limited in scope. The courts tended to frown upon naked restraint, but were less consistent with ancillary restraint.
5. The original purpose of antitrust legislation, i.e., to foster competition that results in lower prices, more products, and more equal distribution of wealth between producers, remains relevant today.
7. b
9. c
11. c
13. a
15. The FTC did not formally have a consumer protection mission until the passage of the Wheeler-Lea Act in 1938. This act gave the FTC the power to combat false advertising for any foods, drugs, medical devices, or cosmetics. In addition to the Wheeler-Lea Act, subsequent amendments to the FTC Act, as well as judicial respect toward the agency, broadened the power and jurisdiction of the FTC.

Chapter 12

1. The term "unfair trade practice" describes the use of deceptive, fraudulent, or unethical methods to gain business advantage or to cause injury to a consumer. Unfair trade practices are considered unlawful under the Consumer Protection Act. The purpose of the law is to ensure that consumers have the opportunity to make informed, rational decisions about the goods and services they purchase.
3. Bait and switch is a form of false advertising whereby the company advertises a product or service and then sells another item in its place.
5. c

Chapter 13

1. International law relates to the policies and procedures that govern relationships among nations.
3. The European Union (EU) is a regional international organization that includes many countries in Europe. It was established to create peace across the region and promote economic, social, and cultural development.
5. a
7. The Principle of Comity states that nations will defer to the laws and decrees of other nations when those laws are consistent with their own, essentially upholding reciprocity between nations with similar laws.
9. b

Chapter 14

1. Laissez faire, as popularized by Scottish economist Adam Smith and British philosopher Herbert Spencer, describes an economic philosophy that markets function best when left to their own devices, i.e., without, or with minimal, government involvement or regulations.
3. c
5. The Securities Exchange Act of 1934 governs secondary markets, or what is typically referred to as the "stock market." In contrast to the primary market, which involves the initial sale of a security, such as through an *initial* public offering (IPO), secondary markets involve subsequent buyers and sellers of securities. One key difference is that primary market prices are set in advance, while secondary market prices are subject to constantly changing market valuations, as determined by supply and demand and investor expectations.
7. d
9. In 1968, the Williams Act amended the Securities Exchange Act of 1934 so that investors could have advance warning of possible corporate takeovers. If someone (individual/corporation) becomes the beneficial owner of more than 5% of a company's stock, that entity must file a Schedule 13D with the SEC within 10 days of purchase. A beneficial owner is anyone with "voting and investment power over their shares." There are a few exceptions that apply, such as qualified institutional investors—large investors who are deemed to have sophisticated knowledge of securities such that they do not need the same level of protection as general investors. Insurance companies, state employee benefits plans, and investment companies are examples of qualified institutional investors who are allowed to report their holdings at the end of the calendar year.

Index

A

abnormally dangerous activity standard, 67
Acceptance, 88
Act of State Doctrine, 146
actus reus, 59, 59
Administrative law, 113
Administrative Procedure Act (APA), 119
ADR, 15
affirmative defenses, 108
agency shop, 104
alternative dispute resolution, 15
Ancillary restraint, 126
Antitrust laws , 56, 126
antitrust laws, 118
appropriate bargaining unit., 104
arbitrator, 22
arraignment, 59
Assault, 65
Assumption of risk, 71
at-will employment, 97
attractive nuisance, 69
audited, 153
Avoiding, 17
award, 22

B

bare bones, 25
baseball arbitration, 25
BBC News. , 149
beneficial owner, 153
Bilateral, 85
binding arbitration, 23
blue sky laws, 158
breach, 92
breadlines, 155
Bribery , 57
Brooklyn Journal of International Law, 39, 149
Business law: Texts and cases , 149
Business Transactions, 23
business trusts, 125

C

California Law Review, 155
capacity, 78
Carter v. Carter Coal Co, 45
case law, 4, 6
categorical imperative, 21
cause of action, 66
Central Hudson Test for Commercial Speech., 49
Chad A. Kelley v. Marsha P. Ryan, Administrator, Ohio Bureau of Workers' Compensation, and Coca-Cola Enterprises, 99
channels, 47
Chaplinsky v. New Hampshire, 49
child labor, 99
Citizens United v. Federal Election Commission, 9
civil, 151
Civil law systems, 147
civil laws, 59
civil matter, 23
class action lawsuit, 24
closed shop, 104
Closure, 20
Collaborating, 17
Collective action, 148
collective bargaining agreement., 104
commerce clause, 44
commercial reasonableness., 91
Commercial Speech., 49
Common law systems, 147
common-carrier delivery contract, 90
Commutative, 86
Company credibility lost. , 33
comparative negligence, 71
compensatory, 61
Compromising, 17
conditional sales contract, 90
Confidentiality, 19
Consensual, 85
Consent election., 104
Consequentialist, 20
Consistency of efforts and partnerships., 37
consistent, 92
Consumer influence., 38
Contest election, 104
Contracting for success, 37
Contracts, 83
contributory negligence, 71
Control, 19
Corporate insiders, 153
Corporate Political Speech. , 48
Corporate Responsibility of the Businessman, 37
Creativity, 19
crime, 23
criminal, 151
Criminal law , 59
criminal matter, 23
cross state lines, 47
crowdfunding, 156
Crown Castle Inc. et al. v. Fred Nudd Corporation et al., 86
cumulative, 92

D

decertification election, 104
Defamation, 65
defendant, 19, 64
delegation, 117
deontologist ethics, 20
destination contract, 90
directives, 117
Disparate impact , 106
Disparate treatment, 106
dissolution, 130
distributive, 16
divestiture, 130
doctrine of sovereign immunity, 145
Doctrine of Sovereign Immunity, 147
dormant commerce clause, 46
due process clause, 50
duty of care, 66
duty to aid, 66
dyadic negotiation, 16

E

e-mediation, 22
embezzlement, 55
Employment Discrimination Law, Visions of Equality in Theory and Doctrine, 110
encumbrance, 89
Enhanced performance for going green., 37
entrusts, 88
ethics, 20
European Union (EU), 145
exclusive remedy, 99

Executive compensation rates during employee layoffs., 33
express warranty, 91
extraordinary ability, 101
F
Fair compensation for employees., 33
fault, 64
Federal and state constitutions, 44
Federal Arbitration Act, 18
federalism, 44
fiduciary, 151
firm offers, 88
First National Bank of Boston v. Bellotti, 48
forced-arbitration clauses, 24
Forcing, 17
Foreign Commerce Clause, 143
Foreign Sovereign Immunities Act of 1976, 145
foreseeability , 67
foreseeable probability of harm, 67
Form 10-K, 153
Form 10-Q, 154
Form 8-K, 154, 154
Fraud , 54
free exercise clause , 49
G
Garnishment, 26
General Assembly, 144
Good faith, 91
Good title, 88
Goods, 86
goods-in-bailment contract, 90
grant of authority, 44
grievance arbitration, 23
Griggs v. Duke Power Co., 106
group negotiation, 16
H
harm , 65
hostile work environment , 107
Houston Chronicle, 34
Hudson Gas & Electric Corp v. Public Service Commission of New York, 49, 49
I
illusory, 88
implies, 92
Improved perception by investors., 37
inaccessibility exception,, 104
industrialization , 114
information, 59
initial, 156
initial public offering (IPO), 156
insider trading, 151
institutional investors, 153
instrumentalities, 47
Insurable interest, 89
integrative, 16
Intentional torts, 65
Interest arbitration, 23
International law, 142
interstate, 54
intrastate, 54
Invasion of privacy , 66
involuntary arbitration, 23
J
Joint Discussion, 20
Joint Negotiation, 20
just compensation, 50
L
Labor, 23
Labor relations, 101
Labor: Studies in Working-Class History, 111
laissez-faire, 156
Larceny, 55
Lawrence v. Texas, 58
Legal considerations., 34
Libel, 65
Liebeck v. McDonald's, 61
Liens, 26
litigation, 15
local unions, 102
loss, 89
M
Malicious prosecution, 65
malpractice, 61
management discussion, 154
material nonpublic information, 152
Mediation, 19
mediator, 19
Mediator's Opening Statement, 20
mens rea, 59, 59
merchants, 86
Miranda v. Arizona, 58
mirror-image rule, 88
misuse, 71
mixed sale, 86
Money laundering , 57
monopolies, 56
N
Naked restraint , 126
National Labor Relations Act, 102
Negative employee relations., 33
Negligence, 65
negotiable, 90
negotiation, 15
NLRB v. Jones & Laughlin Steel Corp, 45, 45, 45
Nominate, 86
non-binding arbitration, 23
non-negotiable, 90
O
Occupational Safety and Health Act, 98
Occupational Safety and Health Administration, 98
offender, 64
offer, 87
Oncale v. Sundowner Offshore Services Inc., 107
Onerous, 85
Opening Statements of Plaintiff and Defendant, 20
organic statute , 113
Organic statutes , 113
Organization Behavior and Human Decision Processes, 15
Outcome goals, 16
output contracts, 88
Ownership, 89
P
pervasive-regulation exception, , 50
plaintiff, 19, 64
police power, 46
Police power, 46
Ponzi schemes , 55
Poor company reputation., 33
pre-arranged trading plans, 153
precedent, 4, 6, 128
preempted, 44
Pregnancy Discrimination Act, 107

prima facie, 106, 127
primary market, 156
Principal, 86
Principle of Comity, 146
Private Caucus, 20
privilege against self-incrimination, 50
probable cause, 49
Procedural due process , 50
Professional behaviors., 35
Property Disputes, 23
Proxy Statements, 154
public law, 113
pump-and-dump , 54
Q
quantity , 87
Quid pro quo, 107
R
Racketeering, 56
rational-basis test., 50
Realty, 86
reasonable person, 66
reasonable standard of care, 66
reasonableness test of reliance, 92
reasonably foreseeable, 67
reasoned, 25
Reciprocity, 148
Recruitment and retention problems., 33
regulatory, 113
Regulatory ethics., 35
Relational goals, 16
remedies, 65
reporting companies, 153
requirements contracts, 88
res ipsa loquitor, 69
restraint of trade, 124
rule of reason, 126
S
Safe harbor, 153
sales contracts, 85
search warrants, 49
Secondary boycott picketing, 105
secondary markets, 156
Securities and Exchange Commission (SEC), 156
Security Council, 144
self-regulatory organizations (SROs), 156
Services, 86
Sexual harassment, 107
Shaming, 148
shanty towns, 155
shipment contract, 90
sideways, 156
simple delivery contract, 89
Slander, 65
Social Security, 100
sovereignty, 145
spam, 57
special relationship, 66
State v. Wayfair Inc., 6
statutes, 63
strict liability, 67
strike, 105
substantial impact, 47
Substantive due process, 50
supremacy clause, 44
T
takings clause. , 50
Talent attraction., 37
tender of delivery, 90
The benevolent halo effect., 37
The legal environment of business: Texts and cases, 149
Thomas-Kilmann Conflict Mode Instrument (TKI) , 17
Title, 88
Tort law, 64
tortfeasor, 64
torts, 64
trade fixtures, 86
trade unions, 101
transparency, 157
Treaty Clause, 143
Trinity Economic Papers, , 149
U
UCC, 86
UN Conference on Trade and Development News., 150
unaudited, 154
unconscionable, 88
Uniform Arbitration Act, 18
Uniform Commercial Code, 86
union security agreement. , 104
union shop, 104
United Nations (UN), 144
United Nations Convention on Contracts for the International Sale of Goods, 90
United Nations Convention on Contracts for the International Sale of Goods (CISG), 146
United States Constitution, 44
United States v. Lopez, 46
Unprotected Speech. , 49
V
Value-based ethics., 34
vendee, 85
vendor, 85
vesting, 101
Void title, 88
voidable, 78
Voidable title, 88
voluntary arbitration, 23
W
warranty, 91
warranty against infringement., 92
warranty of fitness for normal use, 92
warranty of merchantability, 92
White collar crimes , 54
whole, 61
Workers' Compensation Acts, 99
Workers' Compensation Agency, 99
Writ of Execution, 26
Y
yellow-dog contracts, 102
Yielding, 17
Z
zero sum negotiation, 16

www.ingramcontent.com/pod-product-compliance
Ingram Content Group UK Ltd.
Pitfield, Milton Keynes, MK11 3LW, UK
UKHW050950290926
15470UKWH00005B/1748

9 789360 849337